BIG MONEY WITH YOUR BOOK

...Without Selling A Single Copy

BIG MONEY WITH YOUR BOOK
Without Selling A Single Copy

Publishing and Design:

For more information about Trevor Crane or to book him for your next event or media interview, please visit: TrevorCrane.com/media

BIG MONEY

WITH YOUR

BOOK

...Without Selling A Single Copy

For Business Owners, Speakers, Coaches & Consultants

DOWNLOAD THIS AUDIO FOR FREE

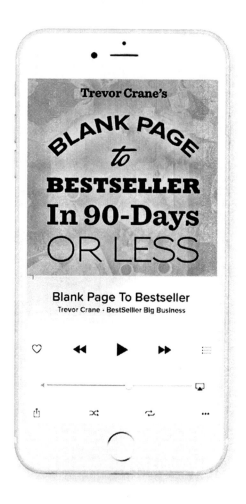

JUST GO TO:

TrevorCrane.com/freeaudio

INSTANT ACCESS

FREE RESOURCES

The interview library, free training &
free consult are available here:

BigMoneyWithYourBook.com

YOUR BOOK IS
ONLY THE BEGINNING

Within the first 12 months after publishing my first book, my wife and I 10x'd our business.

I had no idea how powerful a book could be.

The success we experienced was so explosive, it was like throwing a bucket of gasoline on a campfire.

Writing a book to grow your business is the most powerful and impactful thing you can do to forward your business, cause, mission or legacy.

*Our bestselling author family.

CONTENTS

To my wife Robyn.

You believed in me when I found it hard to
believe in myself.

THE BIG PROMISE

ONE
Why You Should Read This Book

"Success, however you define it, is achievable if you collect the right field-tested beliefs and habits."
—Tim Ferris

As an author, or author to be, you are part of an elite group on this planet.

I assume that, since you've opened this book, you're a published author already, or you're planning on becoming one soon.

Of the nearly 7 billion people in the world, less than 1 percent ever chooses to publish a book. According to a New York Times article, by Joseph Epstein, about how 81% of Americans say they want to write a book.

But, out of every 1,000 people who set out to write a book, only 30 actually finish. And if you then add on top of that the fact that only 20% of people who write a book actually *publish* it, this means only 6 people get published.

I'm also going to assume that you have a business, or you want to have a business, and that you are at least *curious*, about how you can generate income with your book.

Perhaps you wanted to tell your story or share a message. Perhaps you need to establish your brand or make your business more well known in your marketplace. Better yet, you are planning to grow your business and multiply your income along with it.

The challenge is: *most people don't have the faintest clue how to leverage their book into a real benefit for their business, mission, cause or legacy.*

That's what this book is about.

Picture this:

Imagine a world where people approach you, **preprogramed** with the DESIRE to buy your products and services. Imagine a world where it's easier to *attract customers/clients, make sales,* and *raise your fees.*

This reality exists for many people who have books.

The strategies you'll learn in this book have worked with people from nearly every type of business and every walk of life: business owners, entrepreneurs, professional speakers, doctors, attorneys, financial advisors, coaches, consultants, real estate and mortgage professionals, insurance sales people—the list goes on.

Book AUTHORSHIP to *grow your business* and *earn more money* is the most proven, and most powerful path you can take. Period.

Whether it is for; personal promotion, lead generation, gaining media attention and publicity, getting paid speaking gigs, or to promote your cause.

Whether you want to make it to the bestseller lists, or just sell a lot more of your products or services more easily with profound competitive advantage—this book is for you.

Positioning yourself as a *published* author fosters authority, credibility, and trust like *nothing* else. Introducing yourself with a *book* (not a brochure or business card) creates DESIRE for your products and services, rather than resistance.

As an author, you can:

- **GROW** Your Business Revenue

- **EARN** More Money

- **ADVANCE** Your CAUSE

- **LIVE** a legacy and LEAVE a legacy

And here's the even BETTER news ...

You *don't* need to sell a single copy of your book to grow your business and cause.

You *don't* need to wait many months or years to see RESULTS.

Having a book is like becoming an *instant celebrity* in your field.

However, if you *don't* learn how to *leverage* your book to grow your business, you're going to be mightily disappointed.

For most people a book is not what makes you money, it's the business behind your book that brings you the greatest rewards.

How To Use This Book

This book will teach you the exact principles that people like you are using to make money with their book to expand their impact and to change the world.

You have two choices: you can try it the *hard* way, or do it the *easy* way. The hard way is you go it alone. The easy way is to learn the shortcuts and get some help.

I tried going it alone and doing it myself, and it took me over 20 years to publish my first book.

First, I struggled to get started. Then I struggled to finish writing my book—which I procrastinated on decades, because I felt like I'd wasted my time writing the *wrong* book.

Then I stopped trying. Then I felt bad about myself for giving up. Then I tried again. But without a marketing plan, or system behind my book, I was frustrated and confused.

Then, I tried the easy way. I got a mentor. I followed a system. I got some help.

That's my recommendation. Get some help.

This book doesn't just share success strategies with you about making money with your book. Instead, it shares with you stories and experiences from people who are doing it.

The first section of this book focuses on these examples. You will find that it doesn't matter what business you're in, or want to be in, your book can help you take it to the next level.

From "hotdog" examples, to "sales secrets," to a simple "happiness formula,"—you will learn how these authors are impacting people around the world with their books.

You'll find money-making strategies you can use in every chapter of this book. They will be revealed in subtle ways in each interview, and are up to you to uncover and then implement. Not all of the strategies discussed will be ones that you are ready or willing to use. But for those who are ready and searching for "the secret" I have no doubt you'll find many that resonate with you in these pages.

The Secret Speaks To Those Who Listen

If you are ready to put them into use, you will find valuable insights in every chapter. If you're not ready yet, hopefully you'll find something that will light a flame of possibility inside of you, that one day you will not be able to ignore.

These money-making strategies have helped people make fortunes, and impact the lives of millions of people around the world.

This book outlines multiple paths for you.

Pick one and implement it.

In the "PROOF & POSSIBILITIES" section of this book, you'll learn about the interviews I did with five of my favorite people. Instead of *only* giving you my insights and systems, this section focuses on giving you access to authors who are currently having *phenomenal* success with their books, and leveraging them into the growth of their business.

Soon, you'll meet:

1. **Ben Wilson** - Find out how a book and hotdogs saved his life. Ben will share with you how his book helped him earn **$53,000 in** *45 days (with just an $8 course!). If he can do it with hotdogs, imagine what you can do.*

2. **Ryan Stewman** - Discover how he used his book to go from (-$100,000) to generating over **$1.7 Million dollars** in a single year.

3. **Ilona Selka** - Learn how Ilona used her books to **earn more money in a WEEKEND**, than she used to earn in a year.

4. **Anil Gupta** - Uncover secrets to **immediate happiness and success** with CELEBRITY clients like Sir Richard Branson, Tony Robbins, Mike Tyson and more …and who is using his book to impact the lives of hundreds of thousands of people around the world.

5. **Pat Petrini** - See how Pat and his partner are making pretty good money **($18,000/month and growing)** from "book sales." Pat is an anomaly in this book—he is my lone example of someone earning more from *book royalties,* than the business behind the book. *But I think you'll also see the bigger vision, and BIGGER opportunity, that exists beyond his success.

I'll summarize the takeaways and the MONEY MATH, so you can better understand how to position and price your products and services, to explode your business growth and make 6-7 figures with your book.

In these interviews, we will also debunk the myths and pitfalls that you want to know and will definitely want to avoid, so you can use your book to make more money.

This book will:

- *Save you time*

- *Save you money &*

- *Save you heartache*

You can get access to all of the interviews, including the transcripts, and audio and video downloads by signing up at: BigMoneyWithYourBook.com

Putting This Into Action

In the "PUTTING THIS INTO ACTION" section of the book, I will give you the four fastest and easiest MONEY MAKING METHODS you can quickly put into action.

So here's what you should do next:

Grab a pencil, take notes and go for it!

No excuses.

-Trevor

*Helping you take your life and your business to the next level.

$16 Million Dollars

My nine year-old daughter, Phoenix, believes in magic. She also believes in Santa Claus, as do I by the way.

A few years ago, she got a gift that made its way to our house on Thanksgiving Day. It's a little magical visitor from the North Pole that apparently works for Santa all year round. (*"He's making a list, and checking it twice; gonna find out who's naughty and nice!"*)

This little visitor was sent by Santa to keep an eye on my daughter, and report back to him, in the days leading up to Christmas.

Maybe you've heard about this little phenomenon called an, Elf On The Shelf.

Fortunately, he came with a book that described the miracle for us—it even outlined the rules that this little elf has to live by, to maintain his magic.

In short, the kids are not allowed to touch him. And since he's magic, he will periodically move about the house when no one is looking, or when everyone is asleep.

During these times he can become quite mischievous.

My daughter named her first elf, Floodle.

Phoenix loves him. No, I mean, LOVES him. She gets very excited for him when he arrives on Thanksgiving. She speaks with him daily while he's here. She writes him notes. She discusses her Christmas wish-list with him. She buys him special clothes. It's quite a big deal at our house.

As Christmas day nears, and it's nearing time for him to leave, Phoenix gets really sad—she doesn't want to see him go. So before his departure, she made us get him a reindeer (that he could ride before heading off on his long journey). This very specific "Elf On The Shelf" reindeer got to stay behind, after Floodle went back to work with Santa at the North Pole.

That was the first year.

The second year, Phoenix conned her grandparents (who are Jewish) into buying her a second Elf On The Shelf. Apparently there are girl elves too. Who knew?

Her name is Rose.

She also came with a book. Which was identical to the first book, but with a girl elf instead of a boy elf. She, of course, needs clothes. She has a suitcase, special outfits, and shoes, and her own reindeer, etc., etc. But it didn't stop there.

A third Elf On The Shelf, named Chip, now graces our house from Thanksgiving to Christmas, and those little elves get into all kinds of trouble. They eat sweets, they drink hot chocolate, they get cuddly with my daughter's other dolls and stuffed animals. They even wrapped our toilet in wrapping paper.

I'll tell you a little secret. We're not the only crazed family who has these little elves and all the gear that goes with them. By now, you may have made the connection between how powerful a "book" can be, when there's an entire marketing plan and business behind it.

Listen to this sleigh ride to success:

Since its launch in 2005, this Christmas tradition has snowballed from a cute poem, written in a little book (*The Elf on the Shelf*), into a multi-million dollar franchise.

As reported in FORTUNE magazine, on December 12, 2012, year-over-year growth has averaged 149%. Sales hit $16.6 million in 2011. (To see photos of what my daughter's elf shenanigans, go to: trevorcrane.com/ elf-on-the-shelf.)

Not too shabby.

Question for you:

How would it help your business, if a major TV station did a story about you and your book?

Well, not only was The Elf On The Shelf featured by CBS, but a helium-filled Elf On The Shelf balloon floated through Herald Square during Macy's Thanksgiving Day parade.

[Read more about this story in the BONUS CHAP-TERS section: *The Elf That Stole Christmas.*]

This is where the money really starts kicking in...

The Elf On The Shelf costs $30. We have three. Add up all the clothes and gear, and extra stuffed reindeer, and we're easily $300+ into this little guy.

If they didn't create all that "extra stuff," behind the book, there's no possible way for them to have had the impact and created the income we're talking about here.

Our job as authors is to leverage our books into our most powerful marketing tool, so it becomes a money making machine.

I hope you agree.

PS: If you *haven't* written your book yet, check out, *How To Write The Right Book Fast.* I'll ship a free copy to you: trevorcrane.com/writeabook

(I bought it for you, all you have to cover is shipping.)

THE BIG PROBLEM

TWO
Why You Should STOP Reading Right Now

"Build it, and they will come" only works in the movies. Social Media is a "build it, nurture it, engage them and they may come and stay."
—Seth Godin

f the "end goal" for your book is to **sell as many books as you can...** you might as well STOP reading this this right now. The advice and strategies you'll learn in this book, won't be of much help to you.

You must understand that for most people, the best success path for your book is not to try to make money by *selling* your book.

Now, many people don't like to hear this. I also know I'm going to get grief from people who make their living selling books. So, if you make your living on the proceeds from *actual book sales*, as I said, this book doesn't apply to you. *(Or possibly what I'm about to say, and the whole premise of this book, would be even MORE valuable to you... But what do I know?)*

Here's why, and let's begin this with total transparency.

Most people don't make a lot of money *only selling* their "book." Why? **Because most books only sell a few copies.** But even if you sold a few *thousand* copies, it's not exactly big money.

Let's do the math.

How much will people pay for your book?

$10? $20? How many books does the average author sell?

According to Quora, the average number of sales for books in the U.S. is less than 250 copies per year and less than 3,000 copies over its lifetime.

So let's say, 250 sales x $10 = $2,500 (Not a huge windfall).

In fact:

The worst way to make money with your book is by *selling* it.

Even if you find a "traditional" publisher to publish your book, and they give you the ever-coveted *book advance.* Even if you self-publish.

And, no it doesn't matter if you plan to sell your book *online*, *offline*, in *bookstores*, or become a *bestselling* author.

Your chances of making enough income to support your living, from your book sales *alone*, is slim to none.

Prepare yourself for the real story.

- When it comes to *selling* your book, you've got some significant competition.

  Approximately 300,000+ books are published every year. Add this to the nearly 130 million books that already exist, (or 129,864,880, to be exact—according to Google's advanced algorithms).

- Very few non-fiction books will ever become big sellers.

  The Codex Group revealed that only 62 of 1,000 business books released in 2009 sold more than 5,000 copies.

- Your chance of getting your book to reach a bookstore shelf is less than 1 percent.

  There are thousands of book titles competing for the limited availability on a bookstore shelf. With the over 250,000 business books currently in print for example, even book *superstores* only stock 1,500 titles, while small book stores usually have space for less than 100.

- Bookstores *only* carry books on consignment.

  This means that if your book doesn't sell well, they can return your book to the publisher with ZERO payment due.

- 35 percent of all books published will sell at ridiculous discounts or never sell at all.

  As evidence, you can look in bookstores for the "markdown" table or other displays of books offered at slashed prices. Many of these unsold books end up in the trash.

What's The Solution?

I'll say it again.

The most *lucrative* source of income comes from what is *behind* and *beyond* the book. Or, what I like to call the *business* beyond your book.

Perhaps the best way to approach the solution is to ask YOU a question:

"What is the END GOAL of your book?"

Did you publish a book to increase your income, grow your business and expand your influence? Or, are you publishing so that you can sell books in a bookstore?

You see, once your book is done. You've got another problem: *"What are you going to do with it?"*

This is a critical question. Once your book is completed, *what's next?*

If you're reading this book, then I'm guessing you know the next part. You want your book to make you money.

If you intend to use your book to generate new leads and customers and develop income for your business, then you're reading the *right* book. You see, some of the most successful authors today don't view their book in the traditional sense of it only being a "book."

Instead, they see their book as a valuable marketing asset, and a foundation for expanding their business. *"Selling"* books matters little to today's most successful authors. Here's why: they know that with a good strategic play, a book can generate multiple streams of income for their business.

Your book can expand your client base, and sell more of your products and services. Your book can also be *re-purposed* into a variety of *additional* products and services.

Your book can level the playing field, and put you on-par with the so-called *big* players in your marketplace.

Your book can provide you with the name recognition you desire in your chosen niche, and help you elevate loyal customers to raving fans and passionate *advocates* for your mission, or cause.

Your book can help you change the lives of your readers.

Successful authors know that this all amounts to far more than any royalty check earned from book sales.

Your goal as a savvy business owner and author should be to unlock as many income streams, and powerful ways to impact more people as possible. If you're not sure how to do this yet, relax, that's why you're here.

You're about to learn how to leverage your book to build you a stronger business and a better brand that will help you generate more income, and make a great impact with your message.

Your book is only the "beginning."

"What If My Book Becomes A Bestseller?"

Most people think that once that happens your book will just *take off.* They believe that you'll be automatically in-demand for interviews, and people all over the world will just magically come buy your stuff. You'll be famous.

Wrong.

"If you build it, they will come." Only worked for Kevin Costner in the Field Of Dreams. (And "Shoeless Joe Jackson" is probably not your target audience.)

I know of two cases where #1 *New York Times* Best Selling authors, who also got their 15 minutes of fame on the Oprah Winfrey Show, were still struggling financially.

So much so that, that they hired one of my mentors to help them properly market their books, and build the **business behind** their book.

What he shared with them, is exactly what I'll share with you.

What If?

Imagine if Oprah interviewed you, or that Ellen DeGeneres interviews you on her show…

What would that do for your business?

Wouldn't it be wise to have a way to *capitalize* on all that new attention you would get? Because, with no products and services behind all of that attention, you might just be left looking in the mirror and wondering what the heck just happened.

Thinking your book is going to make you big money (on its own) is like being in the music business, and thinking you're going to get rich selling *records*.

Your book is there to help you expand your reach, your influence, and your *profit*. Without profit, how can you expect to pay for the *marketing* necessary to promote you, and your book, and your brand?

As my wife, Robyn, sings from the rooftops, "When you make more money, you can help more people."

Ever hear of the best way to help poor people?

Don't be one.

THREE
Stop Chasing Clients

"The mediocre mentor tells.
The good mentor explain.
The superior mentor demonstrates.
The greatest mentors inspire!"
—Lucia Ballas Traynor

nstead of chasing clients, give them a reason to come to YOU.

When you become an author, you maximize your LEVERAGE, and increase your opportunities to: promote your message and your business, create POWERFUL "lead generation magnets" (that you can use to advertise your products and/or services), secure FREE publicity and MEDIA attention to promote your favorite "cause" or "mission."

It can be for fun or fame or fortune or fulfillment... or your legacy.

It is THE most proven, most powerful ACTION a person can take!

Your Book Can Become Your Most Powerful Marketing Tool.

Casting yourself in the role of a published author fosters authority, credibility, believability and even celebrity like nothing else.

Being introduced as a book author (not a salesman) and introducing yourself with a book (not a brochure) creates INTEREST in place of resistance.

The position of EXPERT ADVISOR is more easily commandeered by the book author than by anyone else.

What can a book do for your life and your business?

It's time for you to find out.

The Chinese Bamboo Tree

Maybe you've heard this story before?

Like any plant, Chinese Bamboo requires nurturing. It requires water, fertile soil and sunshine. But, there is something amazing about Chinese bamboo and the way it grows. Did you know that there are no visible signs of growth for 4 whole years?

Yes, once you plant it, you need to water it. You need to nurture it, and fertilize it every day. But nothing happens the first year. Repeat the same process year two, and still nothing happens. In fact, there are no results for 4 long years.

But when it's ready, what happens in year five is explosive. One morning you wake up and see a small bamboo sprig. The next day, there's an even bigger one. Within 6 weeks, it grows 80 feet or more (holy cow!).

When I first heard this story, I was stunned – really? Yes, this is how Chinese bamboo grows.

Had the tree not developed a strong unseen foundation, it could not have sustained its life as it grew. The same principle is true for people.

People, who patiently toil towards worthwhile dreams and goals, building strong character while overcoming adversity and challenge, grow the strong internal foundation to handle success. The get-rich-quickers and lottery winners usually are unable to sustain unearned sudden wealth.

Had the Chinese Bamboo Tree farmer dug up his little seed every year to see if it was growing, he would have stunted the Chinese Bamboo tree's growth—as surely as a caterpillar is doomed to a life on the ground if it is freed from its struggle inside a cocoon prematurely. The struggle in the cocoon is what gives the future butterfly the wing power to fly.

The same concept applies to human activities—tension against muscles, as we exercise, allows them (our muscles) to strengthen (while muscles left alone will soon atrophy).

It's Your Time

You're ready. Your business is ready. You've already done the hard work. You've worked on yourself. You've worked on your business and your brand.

And, since you're reading this, it means that you're not *yet* using a book to explosively grow your business. But get ready, because the time is *now*.

I like this metaphor of the Chinese bamboo tree, because I think it accurately represents the rapid growth my wife and I experienced when we first published our books. We'd already done all the hard work. We worked on ourselves. We worked on our business. But when we finally had our book, it was as if all that *watering* and *nurturing* finally paid off.

It was pretty extraordinary. In a 12-month period of time, we 10x'd our business.

What was that like?

Clients came to us, ***instead*** of us needing to chase them.

We got asked to speak on stages around the country, in multiple countries actually. We were interviewed on podcasts, asked to contribute to blog sites, and received all sorts of free publicity and media attention.

Finally, people reached out to work with us and we no longer felt like we had to *prove* ourselves to them.

Before we met people, they had a desire to work with us. Instead of needing to *convince* people, we get to CHOOSE whether we wanted to work with them, and select only the best.

When you have the right book, to grow your business, you gain:

Instant Authority, Credibility, Trust & Desire

Become The Hunted,
Not The Hunter

Once you publish your book, you never know where your leads might come from.

One lead came to me from a woman watching the weather channel.

Here's how that happened:

A client of mine had run some ads to promote his business, and his ad was being replayed on the weather channel. He was talking about the successes he had working with me, and the woman heard the story, my name, and looked me up.

Since Google loves Amazon, as it is a very credible source for relevant and powerful keyword and SEO data, one of the first things that popped up about me was my book.

Subsequently, she bought my book, read it and shared it with her husband. Three days later I was on the phone with them, and they hired me to help them with their business.

After that initial meeting, they asked me to *partner* up with them, to negotiate a *multi-million dollar deal* in New York City.

Six years earlier, I was in NYC under much different circumstances. I had just filed a $2.2 million dollar bankruptcy, and moved to the city to be near my 3-year-old daughter. I was starting over from scratch with less than nothing, no credit and very little self-esteem.

To avoid paying for the subway, I carried my 3-year-old daughter on my shoulders, through the streets of NYC in the freezing cold.

At the time, I only owned one old pair of torn jeans. I borrowed a flimsy jean jacket from a friend, and wore layers to fend off the cold. As ashamed as I was, over my state of affairs, I did my best to never let my daughter see my struggles or my embarrassment.

Though I did believe deep down, that my "setbacks" were "setups" for success, it was very hard at times to keep the faith.

It was quite a monumental moment for me that day, several years later, as I was being escorted to a penthouse suite in the Empire State building, to negotiate this contract.

I'm happy to say that opportunities like these find me, and my wife, and my clients daily. We get to choose who we work with, and charge how much we want to charge.

While many of my programs are ridiculously affordable, often my best clients are those who become my high-paying clients. When people pay, they tend to pay attention.

I want to say this again, it's not just me who has experiences like this.

As you will discover in this book, people from all walks of life, with all types of businesses and causes, are experiencing similar, and often *better,* results.

Your PHENOMENAL success is next.

BIG MONEY AUTHORS

POTENTIAL

One day, as a small child, Thomas Edison came home from school and gave a paper to his mother.

He said to her "Mom, my teacher gave this paper to me and told me only you are to read it. What does it say?" Her eyes welled with tears as she read the letter out loud to her child...

"Your son is a genius. This school is too small for him and doesn't have good enough teachers to train him. Please teach him yourself."

Many years after Edison's mother died, he became one of the greatest inventors of the century. One day he was going through a closet and he found the folded letter that his old teacher wrote his Mother that day. He opened it...

The message written on the letter was "Your son is mentally deficient. We cannot let him attend our school anymore. He is expelled." Edison became emotional reading it and then wrote in his diary:

"Thomas A. Edison was a mentally deficient child whose mother turned him into the genius of the Century."

A positive word of encouragement can help change anyone's destiny.

FOUR

Ben Wilson

---

*"We make a living by what we get,
we make a life by what we give."*
—Winston Churchill

almost choked when I heard the title of Ben's book,
Hot Dogs Saved My Life!

But it did get my attention.

Meet Ben Wilson.

(This interview was absolutely hilarious. You should
really, really check it out. Ben made me laugh out loud
about 100 times. A link to see the video interview is in
the bonus section of: BigMoneyWithYourBook.com)

Ben is about as *RAW* of an entrepreneur as you can get.

To sum it up, Ben's book helped him make $53,000 in
45 days (with just an $8 course). And, as he will tell you,
hot dogs "saved" his life.

Ben's the founder of: LearnHotDogs.com and BensCarts.com.

In 2007 Ben was in the furniture business. When the housing market crashed and people stopped buying homes, they stopped buying furniture, and Ben lost everything. That included a multi-million dollar real estate portfolio, private jets, farms, live-stock, businesses... you name it.

From wealthy beyond measure to bankrupt:

Ben ended up in a 2 bedroom apartment, with his 10 children, wondering how he was going to feed his humongous family.

"In one fell swoop, I lost everything. I had been hugely successful in the furniture industry and it all came crashing down...

My wife and I were on food stamps. We lost everything--lost our cars, lost our houses, lost the plane. Everything was gone. I searched around, and was trying to figure out what to do. And I'm not, I swear to God, I'm not pitching on how to get into the hot dog business. But Trevor, hotdogs saved my life."

Desperate for *anything* that worked, Ben heard about someone making a living selling hotdogs.

"I decided, 'Okay. I got to do something.' Because my kids are greedy little shits and they want to eat every day, and so I had to do something, Trevor.

I'm in little Podunkville, Tennessee, in the mountains, and I read a story about a guy in Texas, or New Mexico, or something, that had saved his house with a hot dog cart, and I was like, 'Shit. If he can do that, I can do that. He can't even speak English.'

My first month I did $8,312 and I was like, 'Yes, yes, yes, yes.'"

Yep, you heard it already, but I'll say it again because I think it's funny, *hotdogs literally saved Ben's life.*

Ben admitted to me, during our interview that he considered taking his life. Not because he was depressed or suicidal, but because when he looked at his life insurance policy and did the math, he figured his family would be better off without him.

But after realizing he could really make money with hot dogs, Ben made it his mission to help others who wanted to do the same.

Ben's business model is brilliant.

He gives just about all of his advice away for free. Often times, Ben just gives his book away for free. But on the back end, Ben offers courses and step-by-step training, to help food vendors make more money than they ever dreamed of.

> Ben writes this on his website: "*This saved my life and it can save yours too. It can literally transform your entire life before the next mortgage payment or next car payment or next electric bill is due.*
>
> *You can learn it all, get started on the right foot, avoid the MISTAKES I made, and be on your way in just days. Can you imagine waking up in two weeks and having a job that you know is going to bring in $200, $300, $400 THAT DAY!*
>
> *You have found the MOST COMPREHENSIVE SITE on the planet about vendors, vending and specifically hot dog carts and operations.*"

Ben has a mission. He lives a life of purpose, helping others and sharing his message. Ben is transforming lives. *WITH HOT DOGS!*

Out of the *desire* to make a difference in people's lives, Ben built a business behind his book *Hot Dogs Saved My Life.*

In my book, *Write a Book to Grow Your Business,* I talk about how important it is to be clear about *your* WHY.

You've got to understand the VALUE and *difference* you want to make in in the world, and in other people's lives. Then you need to communicate that effectively.

Ben is masterful at that. With his book, and his course and program behind his book, Ben just recently earned $53,000 in 45 days.

And Ben is making money while he sleeps. In 2016, Ben earned over $100,000 from the course behind his book. But that's not the end of it.

Ben has leveraged it into more opportunities as well.

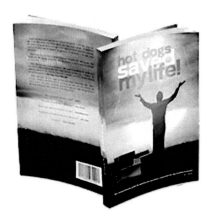

LearnHotDogs.com

I - Main Takeaways

TAKEAWAY #1:

EVERYONE Has Value to Share With SOMEONE.

One of the things you gotta love about Ben is that, he believes if "he" can do it, anybody can.

"People should just be themselves. Just write from your heart. I don't hit everybody with this book. And, you're not going to either. I mean, out of the seven or eight hot dog vendors in the world, that'll probably hit four of them. I'm being facetious obviously...

But be yourself. Write from your heart, and it will take off... I know you've got awesome stuff. But all you gotta do is write it.

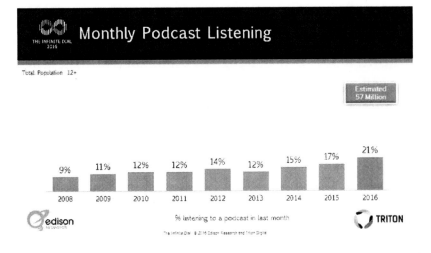

Monthly Podcast Listening

Total Population 12+

Estimated 57 Million

2008	2009	2010	2011	2012	2013	2014	2015	2016
9%	11%	12%	12%	14%	12%	15%	17%	21%

edison

% listening to a podcast in last month

TRITON

The Infinite Dial © 2016 Edison Research and Triton Digital

Maybe you've adopted five kids like my wife did. Maybe you went to prison for 17 years. Maybe you married a turtle. I don't know. Just whatever it is. Write it. If it's something you love and have an interest in, write about it and share it, because this is how information, this is how humanity has grown. This is what saved us from the dark ages. Books, knowledge, and you might not think your knowledge is worth a crap. It is, it is. You know something that you can share. If you've ever given any advice to anybody on anything, write a damn book."

What Ben is saying is don't try to please everyone. Just be yourself. Find out what you have learned in life, write about it, and share it. It MUST be of value to someone.

Now I want to add that you don't just write an autobiography. Nope. You still need to know *who* you are writing it for. Ben did that too. He alluded to it when he said, ‚I don't hit everybody with this book. You're not going to."

I'll talk about this in more detail when I discuss my interview with Ryan Stewman in Chapter 5, but it's important to get clear about WHO you're writing your book for.

Ben knew his target client and wrote so his message could get across to them.

> *"My customer or client is the average Joe, he's me. He's the guy that struggled in eighth grade for three years, right, and possibly married his sister, because you got to remember, we're real close to West Virginia and Kentucky. Trying to be funny..."*

Ben's self-deprecating humor and complete authenticity is infectious. It's perfect for his target market. Hot dog vendors don't need college degrees.

Obviously, they connect with and appreciate Ben. They feel where he's coming from, and like what he teaches. He kept his book format *simple*, and got it done in less than 7 days.

> **"It's [the book] 143 pages and it's not that in-depth.**
> *It's written with my third grade education, so not a lot*

of big words. You're not going to need a dictionary or anything.

*I took a little bit of time each day. I didn't make a rule. Now rules are good for people, but once I started writing it, I had it **completed in seven days, a little less than seven days.***

*...I used a company called ELance, and I went on there and found somebody that could edit it, and proofread it. The gal I found told me, 'You know, there's a lot of misspelling in this book.' I said, **'Well, no shit, honey. I've got a third grade education. That's why I hired you.'"***

She said, 'You're an idiot if you don't do a foreword.' Well, I didn't do one. I just did an introduction, and it's only a half a page long. This wasn't her damned book. It's mine. I did it the way I wanted it."

Ben got someone to help him tidy it up, which everyone should do. The best way to get your book done is to work with a team—get it done right, and get it done fast.

But again, Ben kept it simple. He just went straight to what he thought would be useful for his TARGET READER.

If Ben can use a book to grow his business, YOU can too.

Get clear on what people VALUE you for, and would PAY for. Everyone has his or her special thing. Then write a book about it to the people who WANT and NEED what you must share.

In **Bestseller Academy**, I ask my clients to *survey* their customers to find out what they need. It's simple: If you want to know what people want, and would pay for, you just gotta ask.

TAKEAWAY #2:

When You Add Enough VALUE People Will Buy From You

I was surprised to learn that today Ben's main source of marketing is his book. But he's also put out a TON of other content.

> *"I've got over 800 articles out and over 500 videos out, helping other people start. All for free. What I did with the book though, is I was selling it. I was thinking it was worth at least a million, because you want to make a lot of money off your book."*

I call this, "Goodwill Marketing."

Goodwill Marketing means that *everything* you do to attract people to your business should be creating goodwill—*regardless* if it's free or paid. *Regardless,* if someone chooses to buy something from you. As you can see from Ben's example, when he gives his book away for free, people buy his stuff.

People will keep coming back for more, if you're giving them what they want. And, this further establishes your expertise in your marketplace.

Always be asking yourself, what does my audience want or need? How can I serve them?

> *"My book started that Law of Reciprocity—Where I do something nice for you without the need or desire for you to do something for me. Then, it's almost a human obligation—If you have empathy and an IQ higher than a plant—then you're probably going to want to help that person out later, even if they don't ask.*
>
> *You might send them a birthday card or you might say, 'Hey, I saw you posted on Facebook that you needed a video editor. Here's the one I'm using,' and you set them up with a cool video editor, or whatever. That's how life evolves. That's how humanity evolves. This book ended up being, and it is now, the number one sold book in my industry."*

This is how you build a brand. It's how you build loyalty. And it's done without coming off as cheesy, sleazy, or salesy—because you aren't selling.

Instead, you just focus on giving people what they want.

Here is one of the ways I use Goodwill Marketing.

Podcasts.

I think this is a good time to mention the power of having a "podcast," and possibly a podcast "version" of your book. Podcasts are more popular than ever.

According to Edison Research, the percentage of those who tuned into podcasts grew to over 21% in a single year (between 2015 and 2016). No

"Who" is listening to podcasts? More than you might think.

It's been reported that over 57 million Americans in total listen to podcasts. That's comparable to the amount of Americans who use Twitter. 21% of Americans ages 12 and up have listened to a podcast in the past month. **That's about one in four Americans, ages 12-54.**

The rise in podcast consumption over the past two years correlates with an even larger shift in HOW podcasts are consumed. Circa 2014, most podcasts were being listened to on a computer, which restricts consumption windows.

In 2016, it's a much different story: 64% of podcasts are being listened to on a smartphone or tablet. Listeners gravitating toward podcasts on the go opens up many more opportunities for consumption, including in the car, at the gym, and other computer-free environments.

For these reasons and more, this is one of the reasons I have 2 podcasts.

Simply put, your book and your podcast, if you choose to create one, are extremely good ways to grow an audience and create goodwill with a particular target audience.

You can find my podcasts at: TheGreatnessNetwork. com

II - How Ben Uses His Book to Build His Business & Brand

1. He Grows A List

Ben uses a *piece* of his book as "bait" to get his target customers to stop, pay attention, and capture their email address so he can offer them something in the future.

2. He Sells A "Course"

Ben offers an $8 e-course that teaches people exactly what is in the book

*"I took a piece of the book, one piece. Less than a chapter and created an eBook. Okay. That I gave away. Okay. Then I saw that a piece of **that eBook was so popular, it was getting given away,** because of the wording or whatever. It was working. There's a way to start in this business with zero to no money, basically zero to very little. I decided I'm going to sell that course for $8. **In the first 45 days, I made $53,000 off that $8 ebook.** Then I just offered them the other book almost for free, as a bonus. It took off from there. I had never seen that kind of money for something electronic. I'm used to making a product. Having a sofa made, or whatever, delivering that product, collecting my dollars.*

*I made it once [the $8 product] and it just continues to make money," and it still is now. It's still making money. I'm not even to my year anniversary of that system ... **I'm a little over $104,000."***

*If you already have a book, you can use this strategy and give part of your book away. It wouldn't take you much effort. The content is already there.

In Ben's words, *"Not bad for a hillbilly with a third-grade education."*

3. He Offers A "Membership" Program

Ben's charges $27/month for his membership which includes: video training, cheat sheets, mentoring, and Q&A support.

Again, it's based on the SAME information he shares in his book. He just repurposed it into a different format, and a different modality and learning style.

Within 30 days of this offer, Ben started earning an extra $6K/month.

> *"Make it easy to digest, and then offering the book as an upsell, then offering behind that a continuity program, which I just started, Trevor. The continuity program, which is a membership site, basically ...* **I'm a little over $6 grand a month, and that's all new.** *I'm talking in the last 30 days."*

And again, to give his customers INCENTIVE to join his membership program (he calls it his Street Food PRO Group), Ben gives them 5-days free to try it out FREE of charge with FULL access...

> *"Hey, I've started a group. Street Food Pro Group, and you can join it, $27 bucks a month, but don't worry about doing that now. I'm going to give you five days free. I want you to go in there. I want you to take all the free stuff we have already. Download it. Keep it forever. I don't care if you never come back. Take it all. You can*

get it all in the first hour. Go ahead and grab all that stuff you want, but if you decide you're serious about this business, and you want to see Street Food Vending change your life, save your life, then, by all means, stay. There's no commitment. Leave whenever you want."

This is all enabled by the fact that Ben has a book, and the fact that Ben understands the POWER of building goodwill with his audience.

4. He Sells "Done For You" Products And Services

Ben calls it the "pro-expansion" pack. Where he provides "business consulting" style information (additional 50 pages), credit forms, legal documents, etc. for his customers who want to GROW their food vending business.

"It's offering an expansion on one of the chapters in the book, which the chapter is only like three pages long, about expanding your business. Well, this is the pro-expansion pack. I've written almost 50 pages of information, and credit forms, and hired an attorney to create the legal documents, so they can use them in all 50 states, and they're going to get a package."

It's like offering a "business in a box."

The important thing for you to consider: is what **YOU** might offer your readers, or clients.

Here's an example:

One of my "done-for-you" services is what we call a "Book In A Box." Our Bestseller Big Business team does 95% of the heavy lifting, and for a few select clients, we just build everything.

We strategize with you about the right book, we help you with the title, cover, description, content, and interview you for your book. Then, our team writes it. We edit, format and publish it. We build your website to sell it. We can even create and implement the marketing plan. We can also do the marketing and PR to get you guaranteed media attention with your book.

NOTE: I don't like to take on more than 2-3 of these clients at any one time. Why? **Because it requires a significant amount of time and attention.**

Have you thought about it yet? Have you written down any ideas? It's a good practice to get into, just to brainstorm. Or not. You don't *have* to offer a "done for you" package. It's just a possibility.

Back to Ben.

Another thing I noticed about Ben is how he's continually learning, trying new things, studying marketing and creating new products he can sell.

But, it's also all around the SAME expertise he shares in his book.

It's a good thing to model.

Once you understand what your reader values and needs, you can figure out MANY WAYS to offer them services or products.

5. He Sells High-End Consulting

Ben gained automatic expert status in the food vending industry, because of his book. He built a brand that has created:

- Authority

- Credibility

- Trust, and

- People having a Desire to work with him… at almost any price.

This excerpt from our interview speaks for itself:

> *"Holy cow. I had a guy in July, offer me $25 grand to drive to Raleigh, North Carolina, and spend a day with him, to **help him get started**. That's all he wanted… the bottom line is, all of this [authorship] creates revenue opportunities."*

Would you like to have people SEEKING you out to pay you $25K? Ben appreciated it, but actually he turned it down. That's not a service that he wants to provide right now.

How cool is that? He turned it down.

Since it takes a lot of his time, and it isn't exactly what he WANTS to do, he doesn't do it. (Or, he does it rarely.)

If you'd like to learn how to attract and convert High Paying Clients, I have a book for you. It's called: *High Paying Clients.* In it, I walk you through the exact step-by-step system you can use to sell your high ticket products and services.

It also helps people *obliterate* any limiting beliefs that might be holding you back from getting paid what you're worth. (If you'd like me to send you a free copy of that book, you can find a link at: HighPayingClientsBook .com)

III - "Show Me The Money" Math

Ben offers free or low-ticket items at the front of his funnel. Then, he upsells them into higher price items that earn him more money.

- Course: $8

- Membership site: $27/month

- He manufactures and sells Hot Dog and Vending carts

- He has "done for you" services.

- High-end consulting

Also, notice that Ben's time commitment seems minimal. It's the SAME content. He's sharing the SAME expertise. It's a very scalable business. When one customer joins his monthly membership, or 100 people join, Ben doesn't have to work any harder.

How could you use your book to generate *RECURRING* revenue?

Remember what Ben said,

> *In the first 45 days, **I made $53,000 off that $8 ebook…** I'm not even to my year anniversary of that system, and **I'm a little over $104,000.***

Hot Dog!

Download and listen to the full interview: BigMoneyWithYourBook.com

SUCCESS TIP:

Get a mentor.

One of the fastest ways you can create success is to hire someone who knows how to help you get there.

I spent years, wasting my time trying to figure things out on my own, that I thought I should already know.

Being mentored is one of the most valuable and effective strategies I've found to create rapid success.

Q1: What's something you want, that you don't have?

Q2: Who has experience helping people get that result?

FIVE

Ryan Stewman

"One of the greatest values of mentors is the ability to see ahead what others cannot see and to help them navigate a course to their destination."
—John C. Maxwell

Meet Ryan Stewman, the CEO of Hardcore Closer LLC. He is a bestselling author, motivational speaker, podcast host, blogger and overall *Badass Entrepreneur*.

Ryan has a *no BS* approach to helping people with sales. And today, he offers online and live in-person trainings to help people *master* the art of sales, resulting in higher quality leads, and higher fees for the items people sell.

Of course, one of the big things that Ryan shares in his interview, was how a *book* helped him transform his business from a loss-maker to a profit-making machine.

In 2014, Ryan filed a -$100,000 loss in his business. In 2015, after writing his first book, Ryan experienced an $800,000 gain.In 2016, Ryan generated over $1.7 Million dollars!

To date, Ryan now has 5 bestselling books. As you will see in this interview, he uses them restlessly in the pursuit of his passion and his mission.

The thing I love most about Ryan is that he is really as *authentic* as you can get. He doesn't hold anything back—including some of his specific *business secrets* that he uses to make more money with his book.

Today, Ryan's mission is (in his own words):

> *"I help Salesmen (and women) increase their profits by teaching them skills through* **coaching, consulting, courses** *etc. Many of us in sales come from a broken past or humble beginnings. I'm passionate about my work because I'm one of them. It's my MISSION to help those who came up from nothing and those on the rise to break through the socioeconomic barriers that their past has put in front of them, and help them achieve their goals. I love the sales community."*

Ryan unapologetically works best with what he considers strong "ALPHA" personality type business owners, who want to grow their sales.

I think you'll find his transparency and direct takeaways to be a breath of fresh air.

CloserBooks.com

I - Main Takeaways

Three points that stand out to me about how Ryan uses *books* to further his 7-figure business:

TAKEAWAY #1:

AUTHORSHIP Changes People's Perceptions Of You And Your Brand.

You Gain Authority, Credibility, and Trust.

I have said this before. But it is worth re-iterating so you understand the power of positioning yourself as an author. It is worth you hearing it again from Ryan:

> *"... I went from being Ryan the life coach, entrepreneur (whatever the hell he does guy), into being like, 'Dude, my friend Ryan's an author. He wrote this book and a lot of people are buying this."*

> *It just changes people's perception ... Because idiots don't write books. That's just not how it works. I believe at that moment when I released the book and people saw that I actually did what I was going to do and became an author it changed. I'm not trying to take away from doctors, but it was almost like going through a graduating college with a PhD or becoming a doctor,*

*an MD, or whatever ... **I believe putting the title author in front of your name does the same thing.***"

That's what you get to do when you have a book. You position yourself as an AUTHOR in all your marketing and branding activities, which automatically gives you credibility and authority.

And let's face it, like Ryan said, "Idiots don't write books." And they don't even get close to writing one to grow their business.

So if you haven't already, start positioning yourself as an AUTHOR.

(This is assuming you have a book. If you don't check out the free resources that come with this book, and sign-up for one of my free trainings.)

I share our *step-by-step* proven system that anybody can use to write the *right* book to grow their business.

When you write the right book, you gain authority, credibility, and trust—qualities that aren't easily obtained by other methods.

TAKEAWAY #2:

Your Book Is NOT The Money-Making PRODUCT.

Your book is not your product. It is BAIT to *attract* your ideal customer. To build trust with them. Establish your authority. And invite them to take the next step.

> *"If you were to look at the charts and you saw the trajectory of my business, from where we went from a multiple six figure a year business to a multiple seven figure a year business, you would see that timeline would be almost identical, **almost parallel, to the time that I wrote a book and started marketing myself as an author.**"*

> *Now, notice **I didn't say selling my book. I've sold a lot of copies at this point, but it wasn't about selling my book. It was about marketing myself as an author.** All the sudden, I believe it played such a major role in my business because all of the sudden, I went from being Ryan the life coach, entrepreneur, whatever the hell he does, guy into being like, "Dude, my friend Ryan's an author. He wrote this book and a lot of people are buying this."*

Notice that Ryan emphasized that it wasn't about selling his book!

Though he's sold a lot of copies, the fact is--he marketed himself as an author.

The fact is authorship positions you as an authority. It establishes credibility. It builds TRUST.

It opens the doorway to continue the relationship.

And soon, we will reveal how Ryan leveraged this specific fact, to build his multi-million dollar coaching and consulting business. He is also generous enough to reveal the *specific* figures (the MONEY MATH) behind it.

So stayed tuned.

TAKEAWAY #3:

KNOW Your AUDIENCE.

If you speak Chinese to an English-speaking audience, they won't understand a word you say. They will be confused. In fact, most of them probably *won't pay attention*.

But people do this when they write their books. They tell their *life's* story. They share a lot of *irrelevant* stuff.

It's all good to journal and document your story. Don't get me wrong.

But that's not always what your target client wants to hear.

They want to understand how you can help them.

They want to know why it is important for them to pay attention to you. This is what Ryan had to say:

"See, here's the mistake a lot of people make, they write the book for themselves. I didn't write any of my books for myself. I wrote them for the community. **Just like, Trevor, you're not writing this book for yourself. You're writing this book so that people in the community can have information.** *A lot of people write a book about themselves or they want to tell their story, or whatever the case. We oftentimes think we're a lot more interesting than we really are.* **When it comes to writing a book you want to be strategic about who it is that you want to read the book, and you want to write the book for them."**

I LOVE it!

But Ryan didn't stop there. He clarifies something key here. Especially when it comes to *deciding* what you share in your book.

Part of understanding and knowing your audience, ensures you don't sell fish hooks to mountain climbers. It's all about making sure the *message* that you *market* is relevant:

"Let's say you own a local dry cleaners ... **If you're recruiting other people into your franchise. Or if you're turning other stores around, or whatever, and that's where your main money comes from. Why wouldn't you write a book on how you converted 50 different dry cleaners in the last 24 months**

into whatever it is that you wrote into [profitable businesses]? That way next time you're converting the next one you're like, 'Dude, I make this simple. Here you go. Here's the book. I wrote the book on how to do this.' The book could be Dry Cleaning House: The Book on How to Make Dry Cleaning etc...

It could be anything. But if you write a book on dry cleaning and you try to give it to me, your customer, 'F*ck off.' I'm not going to read a book on dry cleaning. I just gave you 30 cents to wash my damn shirt. Do your job." But if you're making your money from franchising, again, it changes it on who you write your audience to, and that should be how you shape your call to action."

Ryan's example, demonstrates an important point. If you were to write a book for a dry cleaning or laundry business, you wouldn't want to target the customer who walks into the cleaners, and pays a few quarters to get their shirts cleaned.

Instead, you might write a book about, how the OWNER of the dry-cleaning house can make more money with their dry cleaning business, cut costs, push more volume in a given hour, and add enough value to keep customers *loyal* to their dry cleaning house.

Yes, a book is the most leveraged way to grow your business. You've just got to make sure what you are writing about is *relevant* for your ideal customer.

Again, you must figure out WHO you are targeting, WHAT they will want to buy from you, and WHY they should listen to you.

(I hope you're noticing how similar some things are from this interview, as there were in my interview with Ben.)

What's the PROMISE?

In my book *Write Your Book To Grow Your Business*, I share key principles about how to CLARIFY your target customer, so you know what to say to get their *attention*. And what to do and say to get them to take the "*next step.*"

I share how to bake your offering and upsell it into the book, so you can sell them the solution (product or service). It's the PROMISE that will make a positive difference to their life by solving a problem they have, or giving them a BETTER solution than they already have!

I also share the BONUS strategy that my partner and client Steve Napolitan (bestselling author, international speaker, and coach) shares in his book *Capture Clients Close Deals*.

We call it *Survey to Success*.

The best way to find out what your ideal clients need, is simple…

Ask them.

If you haven't started surveying your audience, maybe it's time to start.

TAKEAWAY #4:

DON'T Go For PERFECTION. Go For SPEED & EFFECTIVENESS.

One of the worst ways to earn money with your book, is to waste too much time and effort trying to get it PERFECT, instead of getting it out there so you can make money.

Consider these two stories, and let me know who you'd rather emulate:

STORY ONE: Today, I had lunch with a new client, who has had his book finished for a year. He asked for my help in designing a marketing plan to help him become a #1 bestselling author, and attract new clients.

Instead of self-publishing, he was convinced he needed a traditional publisher. (He wanted to publish his book the "right" way). So he listened to his publisher who paid him a whopping $1500 book advance. For over a year they've been dragging on their feet on getting his book launched. Unfortunately, his publisher now owns the rights to his book, so he can't even design the cover. (By the way he hates the cover.) He's also not yet told his list of nearly 2,000 loyal followers about his book, because he doesn't want to sabotage sales by sharing some mystery date that his book will be released. (He still doesn't know when it will be published.)

STORY TWO: I had my first meeting with another new client, Lisa Chastain, (Lisa is also one of my wife's FEMM Mentorship clients), who decided she wanted to write a book. She wasn't yet clear about the title, or exactly what it would be about, but we made great progress during our first session.

Taking my advice, Lisa left our meeting and immediately posted on Facebook about how she'd just got out of a meeting with her publisher, and that she was going to finally write her book. I asked her to share how much money she'd made in the last 20 days since that post. Here's her answer: "Trevor, I've sold $8,675 from that book post alone!"

I don't know about you, but I'd rather be the second person.

Here's what Ryan shared in our interview:

"The thing is though, I think the biggest sticking point, you probably agree with me, Trevor, is people, they try to perfect their book. They finally get it written. They finally get everything back... they got the cover, and then they start nitpicking the shit out-of-it, and keep trying to make it better. They keep re-editing it or thinking that it has to be perfect and they never release it."

The truth is, if you already have a book, you already have a leveraged tool to position your authority, establish credibility, and build trust with your ideal client.

(This is assuming you have the RIGHT message.)

But let's assume you have that. Once you do, it's up to you to **BROADCAST** that message, your book, to the world.

Every second you fail to do this... is a *wasted* opportunity.

If there is ONE pitfall to avoid... it's this.

I call it the perfection PARASITE. Every time you are addicted to perfection, it *eats* away at your opportunity. Perfection isn't the highest form of excellence, it's the lowest. Because nothing ever gets done.

Ryan puts this well:

*"My biggest thing is, once I finish the book, once I send it to editing, I read it one time and I let it go. **I didn't try to perfect it.***

*I want people to say, **'Hey, you know what? This dude's a real dude that wrote this book. You can tell."*** *You read any of my books, and you can tell I wrote them. You can tell that it is no publishing house that took my shit and cleaned it up.*

You can tell that I literally wrote it. Somebody probably spell checked it for me, and that's even questionable. I think that gives it a massive amount of authenticity though."

Allow me to add to what Ryan shared.

One of the best ways to avoid this pattern, is to work with a team. When you have a mentor and a community to support you, and other people are responsible for their part of the process, things get done.

You can't, or shouldn't, do it alone.

If you want real progress, then work with a team. Especially if what you want is to cash-in with your book.

There is a PROCESS to follow so you get it done right, and get it done quickly.

*"I think in business it's all about speed. As soon as you can put something out **you want to be the first to***

market, so it's all about the SPEED that you can release the book."

II - How Ryan Uses His Book to Grow His Business & Brand

Let's dive deeper in to how else Ryan *leverages* his book to grow his brand and business.

As you probably know, having a book helps you bypass many of your customers' possible objections, skepticism or resistance.

But first, I want to share more details behind how Ryan has leveraged his books into a multimillion dollar business.

1. Ryan PAYS to give his book away for FREE.

What?

He *pays* to give his book away for *free?*

Doesn't that sound CRAZY? How can you make big money with your book if you are *spending* money to get it to them? (Ryan's not crazy.)

Ryan is investing in giving his book away. Because he knows he will make more money than he spends, off the back of it.

"I'm not even selling it. I'm giving it away. Sure, I often have people pay for shipping, which is like $7.00, but that's it. I actually paid to have 5,000 books printed. I pay for the book, they pay for the shipping. Now, I've also been marketing, so I'm paying for the ads to give the book away too. I'm essentially losing money on the front-end of these books. And I've given over 2,000 away as of the time that we're recording this. Probably by the time you're hearing it I'll have given over 5,000 away. It's cost me a lot of money, but I'm making sales on what we call the backend."

How can Ryan do this so confidently?

Well first, Ryan knows what he is selling. He also knows what to *offer* to his readers for them to take the NEXT STEP with his brand and business.

Ryan's current offers are:

- A $297 month membership,

- A $5,000 to 7,000 live event, and

- A $30,000 mastermind

Ryan explains his LOGIC behind doing this:

"Here's how I'm marketing my book: 'Hey, you can have my book for free." Then the book arrives at people's house and they're like, "Oh, dude, this book is awesome.' They take a picture, they post it on social media, and my sales people match their name up...

They [sales people] reach out to them and they say, 'Hey, did you get Ryan's book? [Obviously, we know they got the book.] But they ask anyways, 'Hey, we just want to make sure you got the book. Did you like it? What was your favorite part about it? Did you read it?" There's a few questions that they ask them and go through a sales process we call Catch, and it allows us to upsell them on the backend."

Simple.

Ryan's using his book to broadcast his message.

By offering it for free, Ryan is giving his audience value in advance of making any other kind of sale. As word-of-mouth spreads, more people want a copy of his book.

He is gaining attention for his brand and business.

Here's more about his process:

2. Ryan Upsells People Into His More Expensive Products & Programs

Ryan has his sales people "interview" the people who get his book. Again, they ask what their *favorite* part of the book was, etc. Ryan, or his team, then walks them through his sales system, to find out what the next best investment would be for them.

"Well, if you're a member of the $300 a month thing then you are qualified to come to a $5,000 event. If you don't join the $300 thing you just pay $7,000 for it, but the $300 gives you a $2,000 discount. If you're a member of Break Free Academy Entourage you can come to the live event."

But if you are a member, he discounts this to $5,000. This incentivizes his customers to take the next step.

Once customers attend his event, they get offered AN-OTHER opportunity to take the next step. In Ryan's words:

"Usually when people show up at the live event we up-sell them into a $2,500 a month personal inner circle working thing that we call The Tribe. It's hand on. They interact with me and everything else. **A lot of people that are back there, maybe even some of the people reading this book right now, actually read a free book from me somewhere and end up going through that entire process and becoming a high-level client …**

Again, it's not about selling books … ***It's how you position yourself in the book to be able to become that authority that people trust you."***

Did I forget to mention that Ryan is a 4-time bestselling author?

That's right. He didn't stop at writing just ONE book. Think about it, if ONE book helped him go from -$100,000 loss to an $800,000 profit, why wouldn't he repeat it?

Well he did.

3. Ryan Keeps Writing Books

To date, Ryan has published four number one bestselling books. In 2016, his income increased to over 1.7 million dollars.

Want to guess what he's got planned next?

Book #5.

He got it right once. So he's doing it again, and again, and again.

> *"By the end of 2016…* **we ended up grossing, I think it's 1.78 million in actual collected cash.** *Gross. Not future contracts. Not anything else. I know that, because that's the number that I've got to pay the f*cking IRS taxes on is the 1.78. So that's a bit over double the business I did in 2015.*
>
> *Well, first of all,* **it's over 1.7 million times the business that I had two years ago when I had no books.** *But, it's over double the business from the year that I wrote one book to the year that I wrote two books."*

It's hard to argue with results.

III - "Show Me The Money" Math

How many books would Ryan need to sell to make $1.7 Million?

Let's say he earned $10 per book. $1.7 Million / $10 would equal 107,000 book sales.

Instead, Ryan's focus is to use his book to build his business and earn more money on the backend.

Here's what Ryan noticed:

> *"For every 10 books we give away, we make one sale. So basically we've got 2,000 books that we've given away and we have 200 members who've gotten the $297 upsell. Roughly 10% of the people. That's also a $297 upsell on a 'residual monthly product.' Sure, I'm taking a loss on the front end, but I'll take it every day of the week. Sure, I'm giving my book away, but we're profitable on the backend from the upsells and having my sales team reach out and connect."*

So if Ryan's book only costs $7 to print, how does it cost him $12.00 to give away each book? The $5 difference is the cost of marketing it online. (Remember, he makes the *customer* pay for shipping.)

So for every 10 books he gives away, he makes approximately one sale.

> 10 books x $12 = $120
> 1 sale X $297 = $297
> **$297 - $120 = $177 PROFIT**

But that's just the first month.

What happens the *second* month? Ryan earns another $297. And so on.

What if they stay clients for 6 months?

$297 x 5 months = $1,485 + $177 = **$1,662 Profit**

Ryan's cost? In this example, it's only $120.

What's that *Return on Investment?*

I like to call this LEVERAGE!

And it's just the beginning.

What are Ryan's REAL numbers?

At the time of this publication, Ryan has:

268 members in Entourage (his $297/month program)

65 members in his Tribe (his $2500/month Mastermind)

50 BFA (Break Free Academy) Members per event (his $7000 event) *(FYI: Currently Ryan has a total of 707 in BFA Members.)*

Here's a rough calculation to help "Show You The Money":

268 X $297 = $79,596/month
65 X $2500/month X 12 months = $1,950,000/year
50 X $7,000 = $350,000/event

(Even if my numbers are a little off, it looks like Ryan is going to have an even better year than he did last year.)

Again, here's Ryan's basic message:

"Hey, here's my book FREE of charge.
I bought it for you. (I want you to learn and use all of its invaluable insights and information.) All you have to do is cover the shipping."

He uses his book to upsell his products, services and events.

His book establishes trust. It builds his credibility. And it positions his authority.

All Ryan does next is open up the door to people, by offering even more value, and he SUPERCHARGES his returns.

Sometimes I love math.

So the question is:

What are you going to sell on the back end? How will you use your book?

Will you give your book away for free?

Would you "pay" to give it away even?

What *could you sell* off the back of your book that would MORE than cover the investment to give it away?

All good questions.

What's your answer?

Download and listen to the full interview: BigMoneyWithYourBook.com

SUCCESS TIP:

**Use a team.
Don't try to do it all yourself.**

Here are some benefits of using a team:

Reduced Stress: Sure, you might love doing everything yourself, but overtime this will stifle your productivity and performance (not to mention your physical and mental health).

*It is good to have some pressure sometimes, but having teammates who you can work with you to make your tasks easier will take a heavy load (literally) off your shoulders.

Increased Innovation: Usually the greatest inventions, ideas, and "ah ha" moments can come when you are brainstorming and thinking up new ideas with a team.

Before you start taking on your next task solo…

Go get some help!

SIX
Ilona Selke

"With each dream you manifest, you become a greater, brighter being. Really, our dreams are whispers from our future nudging us to evolve."
—Ilona Selke

eet Ilona Selke.

Ilona Selke is the CEO of LIVING FROM VISION, a company dedicated to helping people live their visions, she also runs the Shambala Retreat Center in Bali with her husband Don Paris Ph.D.(h.c.)

I first met Ilona during an interview on my podcast *Race To 7 Figures* that's dedicated to interviewing million-aires and asking them one question, "If you had to start over, how would you do it?"

If you listen to our interview, it won't take you long to realize, that Ilona is much more *esoteric* and spiritual than my average guest. And Ilona gets things done, and creates incredible results for her clients.

Ilona and her international team of 30+ people, have been teaching (online and live in person) for over 25 years, all over the continent.

She an *international* bestselling author, and lecturer. Her material has been published in multiple languages worldwide (English, French, Spanish, Chinese, Czechoslovakian), and promotes her books, music, self-study online courses, live seminars, and retreats.

Since 1996 Ilona has been using books, as one of the most powerful ways to market and grow her business.

> *"People read books as if they're bibles and once you're published, you are certified as an expert. It's just the number one credibility builder so I thought if I get a book out and explain to people about this course, they would surely buy the course. Great strategy and it worked."*

It helped her get in contact with "big" and influential people in her industry (e.g. she has co-authored with Jack Canfield and Brian Tracy), and it got her into the speaker "circuit."

That put her on large stages to share her message, and *advance* her cause.

Ilona published her first book with a traditional publisher more than 20 years ago. During our interview, we discuss the benefits of both traditional publishing, and why she chose to self-publish her new books today.

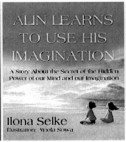
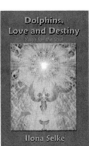

To find more information about Ilona, go to: LivingFromVision.com

I - Main Takeaways

TAKEAWAY #1:

Ilona Creates A Clear VISION For What She Wants.

To use a book to grow your business, you need to start with the end in mind. That simple.

If you wanted to get from location A to B, and you've never been to location B before, you would pull out a map. Or you would Google it.

If your end goal is to *earn more money* or *gain more leads* with your book; then you must know a few things;

1. **What you are going to sell to earn that money.** Because you already know that selling books themselves won't likely lead to massive income.

2. **What you are going to write about.** If you give your readers *the wrong book,* then you waste your time and effort for little to no return.

3. **What your vision is.** It's important that you get clear on the quality of life you want to live, so you can design a business to support it.

There are steps to take to get from *blank page* to *your awesome* book in 90 days or less! You can go to Trevor-Crane.com and download your FREE audio training on this.

> *"The very first thing I would say before you do anything is envision where you want to be and the end result. You have to have a feeling of what you want to accomplish. Is it 10 people you want to reach, is it a million? Whatever the goal is, it's got to be a sizable number and then the venues, the avenues of how that will happen will come to you."*

Of course, it comes down to taking action too. Luck comes from preparation. It pays to do the hard work!

But first thing is first, you do have to get CLEAR on your vision. Get SPECIFIC on what you want.

After the vision is in place, you must take the correct steps in the correct order to get success.

Success is a result of putting your attention and energies towards the outcome.

> *"You may call it luck because you don't see what we do all behind the curtains but the universe and us were having a dialog constantly. Whatever subconscious or cons-*

cious image and feeling we put out will come back as a manifested form. We don't always know our subconscious thoughts but it's worthwhile diving into that part of us and discover it and create greater success. That's what Brian Tracy teaches, that's what Jack Canfield stands for and it's not a cute and quaint belief, it is that BELIEF that makes the difference."

TAKEAWAY #2:

Ilona Invests To Promote Her Books & Her Business

Twenty years ago invested to help her get access to book stores around the globe. She didn't just sit around and "hope" that her books would be successful, and that people would find them, and read them and love them, and then buy from her. Instead, she invested over $100,000 in marketing and promotion.

It was this investment in her marketing that helped her expand her reach and her audience.

"I think that's absolutely vital to invest into if you want to get your book out in front of people's noses. Also having a sales funnel, having your website, your author's presence, your bio looking good and building yourself up...

*That's what I would recommend. If you can find someone who can help you do the marketing, do the digital funnel building and all that or if you're smart and built that on your own, **you can reach millions of people on your own nowadays** with the digital world if you're savvy.»*

TAKEAWAY #3:

Ilona Uses A Team To Help Her Write, Market, & Monetize Her Book

Ilona now writes her book with a team. She has a book coach and famous co-authors partners (e.g. Jack Canfield and Brian Tracy).

She also uses an editor, formatter, writer and publicist who focuses on growing her presence through media and PR.

Ilona is also growing her team to stay current and up to date with relevant technology, video, social media, new websites, and book selling funnels.

One of the core things she believes, and I completely agree with her, is that YOU are your best "advertiser" or "marketer."

Ilona does not rely on anyone, publisher or agency, to just magically do her marketing and promotion for her.

She still hires people to do this. But the point is, she takes *the lead* on the overall strategic direction. This is very key. Ilona knows how important it is that she *broadcast* her message to the world.

That's how you can really get set yourself apart from your competition. While everyone else is thinking about it, or talking about it, you can be cashing-in.

TAKEAWAY #4:

Traditional Publishing Is Dead (at least it is to Ilona)

It is increasingly difficult to make ANY book (or business) stand out.

Your book will be competing with more than ten million other books available for sale.

Add to that the media, Facebook, Snapchat, the newest smartphone, iPads, and shows like *The Walking Dead* and *Game Of Thrones*... there are more and more things GRABBING people's attention and their time.

You have to get creative.

As I said earlier, Ilona is the only person I interviewed who started with a traditional publisher. Back when Ilona published her first book 20 years ago, she had no internet, no self-publishing platform, and no social media. *Basically, all the opportunities we have nowadays.*

The chance of getting published and broadcasted was slim. You needed an agent, and publishers had hundreds of books to review and assess to whether they'd be winners or losers.

Most got tossed out.

> *"Now, if it had been nowadays, I might have gone the self-publishing route especially, well, with your guidance Trevor. My God, if I had met you earlier I would have jumped on that! But I didn't have that resource. All I had was a traditional publishing route.*
>
> *In 1990, basically there weren't many other options but being picked up by an agent who then represents me to a publishing company, well that's another story and I've had so many people knock on my door and say, "Can you open the door for me to get an agent to look at it?"*
>
> *They have 100 books a day to look at and of course they just toss out most of all of them. Going the traditional publishing working route, you would probably tell your clients is like tedious and likely not to lead to any publication."*

Since the publishing industry has changed so much since 1996, Ilona's she's "writing" her book, and "promoting" her new books differently.

In her words, "*The old days, they're over, the bookstores are dying, let's be honest. They're dinosaurs and although they're very cute and many people still like holding a book, it's a dying art.*"

Today, Ilona self-publishes her books. For most authors, I suggest the same.

How do most books get sold today?

Most books today sell primarily to an author's community.

For this reason, and many others, I suggest you engage and grow your community while you write your book.

Publishers will not help you market your books. First and foremost, they are interested in how many books you can sell on your own. They are in the business of selling books.

It's not surprising that a publisher's favorite clients are those people who can sell a bunch of books.

Publishers shift the marketing responsibility to you, the author.

In recognition of this reality, most proposals from experienced authors now have an extensive section on the marketing platform and what the authors will use to publicize and market their books.

*Yes, publishers can still fulfill important roles in helping craft books and making them available in some sales channels, but whether those books *move* in those channels depends primarily on the authors.

Often times, the *benefit* is not worth the **cost**.

II - How Ilona Uses Her Book to Grow Her Business & Brand

Throughout the interview, Ilona shared key insights as to how to use a book to grow your business and brand.

1. Ilona Uses Her Book To Upsell Her Products & Programs

A book is better than a business card. Think about it. Someone walks up to you with a business card and tells you, "I help people manifest their dreams." (this is to use Ilona's business as an example).

Contrast that with someone walking up to you and saying the same promise, and presenting themselves as an AUTHOR of a book that teaches just that.

Instant credibility, trust and authority.

Once you have those three things in place, people will have the DESIRE to buy your product and services.

So you must have something ready for them to buy. They want to take the next step ... with You!

> *"I always say, if you want to make money with a book, use the book as a brochure. Upsell something, even if it's a novel, upsell doing a seminar, upsell a workshop, upsell a webinar that you do, whatever you do, do more than just the book. Otherwise, you get a dollar per book if you're lucky and even if you self-publish it, you have to have a huge outreach before it even matters.*
>
> *Be creative, think about ways that you can sell something, you can do an online course these days, just go to ... There are so many online course production companies...*
>
> *Whatever it is, just think strategically, what can I upsell? Maybe you run a bed and breakfast. I know one person who saw me and asked me, 'Please help me go through publishing house and ...' I said, 'Well, the book isn't going to get you that much money, but since you have a retreat center, get people to come there.'*

2. Ilona Uses Public Speaking As A Platform

Ilona uses her book to gain media attention. One of the ways to do this, is be invited to *speak* on stage and share your message.

Once you do that, you can sell products and seminars off the back end, just like Ilona did. It allowed her to build a relationship with her audience.

> *"I was a speaker then they thought I was really some-body and other people invited me to their events and speakers and blah, blah, blah. It goes on and on.*
>
> *Once one gets into a circuit then there is a recognition. To get there, you have to get in front of people's noses. These days we are so lucky to have people like you gui-ding us to do online marketing, to do e-book marketing and to get the flash out there. Whether you sell a book or not doesn't matter, people see you and then sign up for your webinars, for your podcasts and then they get to know you and then they want to sign up for more of you."*

3. Ilona Keeps Writing Books

Ilona's not resting on books that are 20 years old to fuel her business.

She continues to write books to grow her business, just like Ryan does.

After all, if ONE book helps to grow your business, imagine what MULTIPLE books can do for your business?

I'm invited to speak there at a conference and then I just published my children's book in Hindi and they want me to do a workshop there, just said, "Please send me the write up so we can help you promote the book there."

... The busyness is because I'm excited, I really have the mission to get this message out to the world that we can create heaven on earth around us.

I love putting feet under everything. I'm practical and I'm a visionary like you said. I love that also you are a man of action and you get people to complete and to become successful. I know one of the persons that has worked with you got to the million book sales I think quickly. Yeah, I love people who have visions and your daughter, you're doing these amazing things for people so I think you are a perfect person to guide people into this online success which is this amazing new platform we have nowadays available that we didn't have in the old days so thank you, awesome, I'll join you."

4. Ilona Has A Worldwide Marketing Strategy

As I mentioned before, Ilona serves *different markets*. Her books are translated in different languages worldwide including: English, French, Spanish, Chinese, Czechoslovakian, and even Hindi!

You too can do the same.

If you already have a bestseller book that is earning you money, consider translating it and entering different markets too!

> *"I have had super amazing success, the course is even available in Chinese now. I have teachers in Singapore, all over the world, people who are getting results and they keep doing the course."*

III - "Show Me The Money" Math

For those authors who for some CRAZY reason, still want to make money from just the "sales" of your books, note that:

Ilona made 100 to 1000 times more money from selling her backend products and services, than she earned from royalties from her books.

Primarily, Ilona has used her book(s) to grow her list, and offer her; courses, seminars, training, and events on the back-end.

Here's an example:

Ilona made MORE MONEY in a a weekend than she used to in a year.

> *"Let's just say, my very first book got me a royalty of $10,000, a jaw dropping $10,000. It may not be that much, but it will help you through a couple of months, right?*
>
> *But then, at my first seminar at age 30 got me $14,000. In a weekend! All right so the book got me to get the seminar or get me to get the people believing in me that I can teach a seminar. One weekend equivalent to the royalties for one book, I mean, really, where is the math."*

*I want to remind you that I first met Ilona because she is a millionaire.

The foundation of her success one was built upon her "books" and her "programs" that backed them up. **That's powerful.**

When I asked Ilona what she'd have done to grow her business if she *couldn't* use a book, this was her response:

"Ouch, I'd be out of business! Well, maybe not. Let me think… If I didn't use books to drive my marketing, I guess I'd do these days with video.

But, the credibility of books has been so engrained into our subconscious, that I wouldn't want to try to do it with video alone. I think it comes from the olden days when the bible was like 'the' book. There is still something in our culture that says a book is credibility. And if you write a book, or it's written in a book, it's got to be true."

Books work.

Of course, it's not just about the money. Yes money matters, but I think it's more about "impact." Money is merely a measure of that impact. It's like the *adult* report card. The amount of money in your bank, is in direct proportion to the amount of value that you add to other people.

If you don't like the number in your bank account, *your job is to find more ways to help more people.*

Ilona shared a story about a woman whose life changed thanks to Ilona's books.

"In 2002, she bought my book in Germany. As a matter of fact, it's a really magical story. She read my book and for some reason people have told me this, they thought it was a bible to them, they read it over and over.

She ordered the self-study course, she did the self-study course, she had been sick for 17 years and nobody had been able to cure her, no doctor had been able to help her. She just went ahead and envisioned herself in this beautiful green light, strong and healthy and living the life she wanted to live.

Now, fast forward, another year, her mother gives her a ticket to Sri Lanka to an Ayurvedic doctor, the most famous doctor of Sri Lanka.

She goes there and lo and behold, he helps her get totally healthy. She's cured a year later, she keeps envisioning her life using the course again and again and as a matter of fact wrote me just a year and a half ago and said, 'Well you know, my CDs are worn out, do you have a digital version?'

I said, 'You are so lucky we have the app now and we have the course, Living from Vision, you got it.' I upsold her on it, years later to the digital version. She kept working it and she said, 'I'm moving to Indonesia, can I meet with you?' We never were in touch anymore because Indonesia is big...

I didn't follow up with that. Anyhow, my husband and I decided to go on vacation just for Christmas, to go somewhere where nobody knows me. We went to Lombok, we get out the airplane basically... the next day we go to the hotel that I'd booked online.

We missed our turn, we drive by a beautiful, huge sign that says, 'Ayurvedic Clinic and Vegan Food.' We said, 'Let's have dinner there.' We found our hotel. For dinner we go to the vegan restaurant, I come in and say hi, "So you speak German."

She said, 'My name is Daniella.' I didn't even introduce myself and she said, 'Your name is Ilona Selke.' And I said, 'Why yes I am. It's nice to meet you.'"

Download and listen to the full interview: BigMoneyWithYourBook.com

SUCCESS TIP:

Engage your audience.

You must fight the urge to simply put your head down and write your book, without engaging and interacting with your audience.

Instead, you must continually ask yourself, *"Who are you writing this book for?"*

Interact and engage with your audience to make sure you,

1. Write a book they care about, and

2. Create a *demand* for your book in *advance* of it coming out.

In other words, "marketing" your message *directly* to your ideal target market."

This is one of the most powerful things you can do for your book and your business.

Engage your audience and they'll become raving fan clients.

SEVEN
Anil Gupta

"Be so great that you cannot be ignored."
—Steve Martin

*"Be so great that you cannot be ignored. And if you are…
it doesn't matter."*
—Anil Gupta

Meet Anil Gupta.

Anil works with and coaches some very rich and famous folks. Some of the people he's worked with include: Sir Richard Branson, Tony Robbins, and Mike Tyson. (Plus, many more he cannot speak about, to protect their privacy.)

Anil works to help people resolve any blockages to experience overflowing abundance, happiness, and fulfillment.

He is also author of the book *Immediate Happiness*, which has helped him gain all sorts of fame (e.g. Featured on Fox News, and lectured at Harvard University), and impact the world through his; seminars, personal coaching service, retreats, and DVD products.

Thanks to his authorship, Anil has been able to live a life of happiness, and impact hundreds of thousands of lives worldwide.

When I interviewed Anil, I wanted to extract from him the *key principles* that helped him *grow his business* using his book.

What he shared took me by surprise. Especially since it had *little to do* with directly selling or marketing products and services. My interview with Anil Gupta was unique because it was much less focused on the "monetary gain" or "business strategy."

This was very interesting, because I believe Anil is probably the most financially successful of the people I interviewed. *(Since I don't know his exact numbers, I'm only guessing.)*

There are ways to make more money using your book. However, of everyone I interviewed for this book, Anil's approach and our *entire conversation* was more about his purpose, his passion, and his mission to help people.

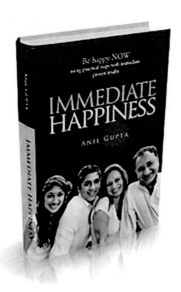

ImmediateHappiness.com

1 - Main Takeaways

In 2008, Anil was on the verge of suicide. That experience helped him reveal his bigger purpose.

It wasn't just about himself anymore.

He started focusing on being of *service* to others. He got CLEAR on his mission, and his pain started going away. He uncovered what he did best, and loved to do most ... transformational coaching!

> *"2008 November, was the worst period of my life. I was on the verge of suicide ... that was the turning point because I realized that I'm here for a bigger purpose. It's not about me. I was focusing about me. In the moment you start focusing on other people, and the moment you start giving, and the moment that you focus away from you, the pain disappears."*

So he focused on that, and found a way to build a business doing *exactly* that. It was about making a DIFFERENCE in people's lives.

It took him a long time get the awareness and the help, that would allow him to embrace what he really wanted to do with his life.

Once he got that "clarity" and "awareness," everything changed.

At the turning point of his life, Anil's wife asked him, "Honey, what do you love to do?" He responded, "Well, you know what I love to do. I love to coach."

His wife asked, "Why don't you coach?" And Anil said, "What about the money?"

His wife responded, "Look, honey, I've never asked you for money. You know that. Just do what you love, and everything will work out."

And Anil did exactly that. He started coaching by sharing what he did with people. This led Anil to speaking on stage in front of over 10,000 people.

> *"The first event was like six people, then 10, 20, 100, 200 ... Recently, I spoke in front of 10,000 people ... mostly Spanish. They did a simultaneous translation. I was on stage for 90 minutes non-stop."* **—Anil Gupta**

After speaking on stage, people started approaching Anil and saying, "Hey, let me pay you for this!"

This was before Anil even had a book.

One of the biggest things I learned from Anil is to just follow you heart.

I know that sounds a little "fluffy," in a book that's supposed to be giving you monetary strategies you can use to grow your business, mission or cause...

But it's the truth.

You heard Ilona say it. You heard Ben say it. I don't think it's *coincidence*.

This is something I really appreciate about Anil and all the people I interviewed for this book. It's also something I tell *all* my *Bestseller Big Business* clients who are in my Bestseller Academy or Bestseller Mentorship programs:

It's important that you find something that lights you up and brings you more happiness and joy.

Or else, why bother?

TAKEAWAY #1:

Define Your WHY. Get CLEAR On Your Purpose.

What's your purpose? What's your *gift* to your customers?

Now, getting clear on your WHY itself isn't just going to lead to instant success overnight. But it'll give you motivation and inspiration to get it done, when the going gets tough. And it will get tough.

But having clarity around your purpose, helps it not feel like work. Instead of "draining" it can be "fulfilling."

Rather than having your book stay as a "nice" idea, it can be out there *making a difference.*

> *"My book was on my desk as a draft copy for one whole year because I was thinking in my head, 'Who am I to write a book? How dare I write a book? Other people are smarter than me. You know, what will other people think of me? You know, will the criticize me?' But at the end of the day, I asked myself, 'Will this make a diffe-rence to one person, 10 people, 100 people?" and said, 'Yes, Anil, it will,' then just get it done."*

Anil is a great example for all of us. *Especially*, when we have a higher purpose or greater desire for the *impact* our book will have in the world.

TAKEAWAY #2:

Don't Be A Perfectionist.

Anil believes, "Every day you *delay* in writing your book, people are suffering without it."

Couldn't agree more.

There are people out there who want and need your expertise. Not to be dramatic about it. But they are, in some cases, literally dying for it.

Say you found a new solution to a health-related prob-lem which was causing great suffering. If you *don't* get the information out to these people, wouldn't that be a disservice to those people?

In Anil's words …

> *"It's not about me, it's about the difference I can make. Every day that I delayed writing this book, someone was in pain. The secret is to serve. If you serve other people not wanting anything back, that's where you get the biggest success."*

TAKEAWAY #3:

Money Is An Exchange of Value.

Anil wrote a book that he was passionate about that would serve people, with seemingly zero desire to "make money." Anil believes that money is simply energy. And it all depends on what energy you are giving out.

> *"I'd just like to share: a man's wealth is determined by his possession-less self. **A man's wealth is what he has left when you take away all his possessions.** If you take that into consideration, you can assess how wealthy you are."*

Anil had a clear intention. To give value. The best way to give value is to *understand* what people want and need, and then *give it to them*.

TAKEAWAY #4:

Give Your Gifts Away Without Expecting A Return.

Anil's happiness formula is "G" cubed: Give Gratitude & Growth.

- **1st G: GROW**. You must grow emotionally, physically, mentally and spiritually. It is *always* a positive return if you invest in yourself and your business.

- **2nd G: GIVE**. You must give—your gift, time, love, energy, passion and money. This is a the law of reciprocity.

- **3rd G: GRATITUDE**. You must have gratitude for what you have and not resent for what you don't have.

In the interview, Anil extended the discussion of his 3G formula, sharing his *3 TIPS* to succeed at anything you do in business and life.

Here is Anil's advice:

1. Write Down 50 Things You Are Grateful For.

"Normally I would ask for 100, but write down 50 things you're grateful for. You know, the air. You know, we 'poop' in water that other people from other countries would 'love' to drink. **We take things so much**

for granted. *Water coming out of a tap, we take it for granted. The air that we breathe, the house that we live in is safe, and it's not being bombed, or you're not getting people trying to break in."*

2. Perform 5 Random Acts of Kindness.

"You know, smile at someone. Say thank you. Ring up a friend and say, "Hey, man, I want to thank you for your friendship. I love you." Ring up your father or mother and thank them. Do something that will change someone's life. It's the smallest thing. Opening a door could change someone's life. We have no idea the impact we have on other people's lives. Just do those two exercises, and I promise you, just be aware of the feeling that you get from doing them. It'll become addictive."

3. Ask the ONE You Love, "What is it you want from me?" and "How can I serve you?"

"I think the tipping point was when my wife said, "I don't care about the money." That was the tipping point, because I felt I was a failure to her and kids. She said, "No, that's not what I want." This is another exercise your viewers and listeners can do, is ask the one that you love the most: what is it you want from me? How can I serve you? You'll be surprised at the answers that they get. Communication is the key."
—**Anil Gupta**

II - How Anil Uses His Book To Grow His Business & Brand

Anil said that his book helped him organize and systematize his formula and protocol, for how he helps people. He also agreed that it was a foundational part of his brand, and helped him establish his credibility and authority.

The biggest thing however, is IMPACT. Anil said his book has touched the lives on hundreds of thousands of people. It seems that Anil is proud of his book for one reason: it helps people.

Since then, Anil *streamlined* the process for using his book to make more money and help more people.

He offers his book for FREE on his website ImmediateHappiness.com.

Again, he's *giving* it away.

Why?

I know we've covered this already… Authority, Credibility, Trust… etc. But for Anil, the most important part is to just give the gift of his book to as many people who are open to receiving it.

If it creates a desire for people to work with him, he's happy to do so. If not, that's okay too. Anil just wants to help people.

Anil doesn't make 'money' from his book. But he *uses* it to build his business and his brand.

Here's how:

1. **People opt-in to his email list to download their free book.** They do this by entering their first name and email address. Their book gets delivered to their inbox.

   Anil then builds a relationship with them. On Anil's website, he offers *coaching services* to those wanting to take the next step.

2. **His book gets him media exposure.** Anil has been featured twice on Fox News, and has an open invitation to return to speak.

   He even spoke at Harvard twice, and was featured on Sky TV for a whole hour! So Anil's message and mission gets *broadcasted* to the world!

   But how does this earn him money? Simple. Traffic gets *directed* to his website again. There, they download their FREE book by opting in to Anil's email list. And he gets to offer his coaching services.

   *"I don't know how many books are sold, but I have a free download on my website. **I mean, because I really, I just want people to read it.***

From that book, I was able to get on to Fox News twice. I have an open invitation to go back. I spoke at Harvard twice. I've been on Sky TV for an hour, and some other TV programs. I've done numerous podcasts, radio interviews, talks, speeches, Facebook, Facebook Live. Really, it's been able to reach so many people.

It wouldn't have happened without this book. It would not have happened."

III - "Show Me The Money" Math

During our interview, I probed Anil for specifics, and to discuss numbers and money.

However, all during our nearly hour long conversation, Anil didn't want our contestation to focus on money.

Instead, Anil told me he uses a different currency.

"Well, the thing is this. I stopped using the U.S. currency. The U.S. dollar is no longer my currency. I use a different currency. The currency I use is the currency of love, joy, giving, loving, being present, being caring. **If everyone used that, they would be billionaires."**
—Anil Gupta

I'm reminded of a quote I love by the late, great Jim Rohn, "You are the average of the five people you spend the most time with."

It's not really important exactly how much Anil makes, but with friends and clients like: Sir Richard Branson, and Tony Robbins, I think Anil is doing just fine.

Considering that... I may change my currency as well.

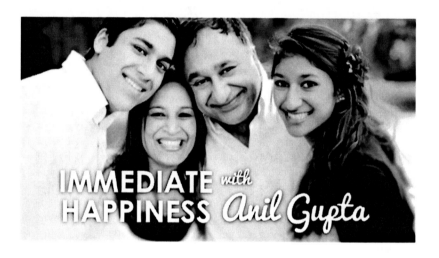

Download and listen to the full interview: BigMoneyWithYourBook.com

SUCCESS TIP:

Celebrate every phase of your book.

Marketing is about communication.

In a crowded market, you need to stand out.

If you're not communicating with your audience they are not thinking about you.

There has never been a time in history when we have had the ability to connect with so many people so effortlessly.

You can easily leverage the POWER of being author, and your book, by merely SHARING the "progress" of writing a book, or the next phase or version of it.

Talk to people about your book.

Don't be shy.

EIGHT
Pat Petrini

"A mentor is someone who sees more talent and ability within you, than you see in yourself, and helps bring it out of you."
—**Bob Proctor**

M eet Pat Petrini.

Pat is an entrepreneur in the REAL ES-TATE industry. He got started in direct sales and networking marketing, where he was known as a TOP producer and consultant.

Pat is the #1 bestselling CO-AUTHOR of the book *The Miracle Morning for Network Marketers.*

Pat has also making some nice "book royalties" every month, since his book launched in September of 2015.

In January 2017, Pat's book royalties were $18,000, and growing every month. (Pat shares that with his co-author and partner, but we'll talk about that later in this chapter.)

Yes, Pat's making some pretty decent money with his book. Yes, his experience *contradicts* what I have been talking about in this book so far. *(Which is one of the reasons I like having him in here.)*

However, Pat *isn't* just relying on book sales for income.

As you will learn from this interview, he is STRATE-GICALLY *not selling* anything (or much) off the back of his book YET, so he can make better and BIGGER BUSINESS GAINS in the future.

You'll love it.

Today, Pat spends most of his time in the REAL ES-
TATE industry, as a trainer, speaker, and entrepreneur
who shows people how to create significant income in
real estate without having money, credit, and prior experience.

> *"A few years ago, my life fell apart financially, and I was
> able to turn things around completely using a shortcut
> that I learned in real estate. Today, in addition to ope-
> rating a successful real estate investment company, I've
> developed a program to show people how to create sig-
> nificant income in real estate with no money, no credit
> and no experience. It's called The Real Estate Shortcut."*

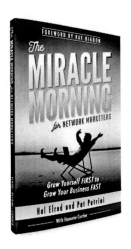

PatPetrini.com

I - Main Takeaways

As I said, Pat is unique among the people I interviewed for this book, primarily because his book 'itself' makes some pretty nice money. The business 'behind' the book, is a long-game for Pat that has a huge potential upside.

The three things that stand out from our interview are:

TAKEAWAY #1:

The Power Of Co-Authoring A Book (with the right partner)

Another thing that was unique about my interview with Pat, is that he had not every really considered being an author, until he was approached by a friend of his, who asked him to co-author a book with him.

Pat's friend of 15+ years, Hal Elrod, approached Pat to co-author a new book in his "Miracle Morning Book Series." At the time of this publication, Hal has 2180 phenomenal reviews on Amazon, with an average of 4.6 out of 5 stars.

As Pat put it in our interview:

> *"I hadn't really planned on doing, but I thought it'd be a great challenge. The other thing was I saw the success that was already occurring was the Miracle Morning Platform and I thought it would be dumb not to be able*

to create what I thought was a quality book and have an already existing platform to watch it on. I said, "Yes," right away and started figuring out how to write a book and that was quite a process, but, yeah, that's I guess the basics of how it got started."

Pat immediately accepted the offer.

TAKEAWAY #2:

The Power Of Clarity & Writing Your Book Quickly

Pat struggled while trying to write his book for nearly 6-months, until he got "clarity" about the project, and his system to create it.

When he finally figured it out, Pat got his book done— fast.

Once Pat found this "clarity" he created the outline for his book in 2 hours, and wrote the main manuscript by speaking into his phone, while taking a long 4 hour walk around his neighborhood.

In 6 hours he captured the first draft of his book, compared to the previous 6 months of wasted time and energy where he seemingly made no progress.

"After I got that outline done, I went on a walk for literally about four hours, four and a half hours, with my

*iPhone in hand. The default voice recorder app that it's got on there just pulled up and I was walking around the neighborhood with my outline in front of me speaking into my iPhone and recording it. I recorded each of the different chapters. **If you make a mistake, you just keep piling through when you're dictating like that. We took those dictations. I sent those to a service.** I think I used speechpad.com, I'm pretty sure."*

Within 2-3 months, Pat's book was complete.

"Eventually, I finally landed on a process that worked really really well for me that I'd be happy to go into if you want me to. Once we landed on that process, then I think we had the book pretty much from the beginning to end in maybe three to four months, once we got the right process the work for us ..."

I love hearing stories like this.

You can write a great book. You can create something that you care about, believe in, and get rave reviews, WITHOUT wasting time and WITHOUT having previously ever written a book. You can do it quickly.

What's needed, just like Pat said, is a PROCESS to get it done. A SYSTEM that is proven to work. One that helps you gain CLARITY on what to do first, what to do next, and so on until you have your book *done*.

In Pat's case, he learned that you must get clear enough to have an outline for your book, so you know WHAT you need to share with your reader.

He then SPOKE IT (his content) into his phone, while walking around his neighborhood.

Once he spoke it, he had it SCRIBED, and could capture his FIRST DRAFT of his book within 6 hours.

When you have clarity, you can get your book done quickly.

Truth be told, I get more than a little geeked-out by what Pat shared, because it is EXACTLY what we focus on in all of our Bestselling Big Business programs.

We focus on helping clients get clear on WHO they are writing the book for, WHY that audience would care about the book, and WHAT they plan on offering beyond the book.

Step by step.

II - How Pat Leverages His Book to Build His Business & Brand

Because of the unique partnership that Pat has with his co-author, Hal Elrod, Pat's main focus is on connecting with and nurturing his ever-growing list of readers.

1. Pat Grows His Email List

> *"Aside from the sales of the book we integrated some lead generation strategies into the book, so the book refers to a lot of bonus material as you're reading it and that bonus material's online and you go and you opt in to access that bonus material.*
>
> *That email list is an asset that we can now use for affiliate marketing as an additional revenue stream... The size of the list is a little over 4,000, probably 4,100, 4,200, something like that."*

What Pat is saying is that people will buy from you when they trust you, and trust that you can help them. Today, Pat's book has accumulated over 4000 new leads. This isn't a huge list, but Pat has been very careful to nurture this list, and he is happy to report that they are a very responsive list and are very engaged.

The larger this list grows, the greater Pat's opportunity to make new sales. Pat's job is to support this list. To connect and communicate with them, and find more and better ways to serve them.

Every now and then, Pat will offer this group something fro them to buy, using *affiliate marketing.*

What is affiliate marketing? Where you find a vendor (someone who provides a product or service), and you help them sell their offering to your list. In exchange, the vendor gives you a percent of the sales.

The great thing about this strategy, is that Pat doesn't waste his time creating his your own product or delivering some new service. Instead, he simply offers his list, (who he has a trusting relationship with), if they want something "cool" that he just found them.

I think it's great.

Now, let's return to discussing more about Pat and his book.

Pat's co-author, Hal, is responsible for all of the ongoing marketing that they do for the book. He's a regular guest on podcasts, radio shows, blog sites, and other media. Hal is also an extraordinary speaker, and uses his book series, and stories to leverage speaking engagements around the world.

As Hal continues to BROADCAST his message, Pat & Hal continue to gather more and more leads. And just like Ilona experienced, speaking engagements allow you great opportunities to sell your products to your audience.

2. Pat Used A Pre-Launch Team

You may be picking up on the "theme" of our authors, in that their success does not hinge on any ONE element, or any ONE person. Pat wrote his book, using a team. He markets and promotes his book, using a team. He considers his readership, part of his TEAM.

I honestly believe that, "Nothing truly great was ever created alone."

> *"Teamwork is the fuel that allows common people to attain uncommon results."*
> *—Andrew Carnegie*

If you want to super-charge the launch of your book, you might want to model what Pat shared with me about having a prelaunch team.

Originally, Pat's goal was to get a team of 100 people who would agree to help promote the initial launch of his book.

In order to attract and incentivize this launch-team, Pat and Hal (and the rest of his team) offered their friends, family and followers numerous bonuses that created excitement, and anticipation for the upcoming book.

They also gave them an advance look at the book, and connected them in a private Facebook group, to build momentum.

In the end, their prelaunch team grew to over 900 people. This team agreed to: 1. buy the book, 2. talk about and promote it, and 3. leave a review on Amazon.

This is how Pat puts it:

> *"As far as the launch goes, we did this prelaunch team. We offered a bunch of access to all the free bonus content, early access to that. We gave people a free digital version of the book for being in the prelaunch team ...*
>
> *We made the book available on Amazon on a certain day but secret at the lowest price we could possibly list it, so that anybody in the prelaunch team could get access to the physical book as well at the lowest possible price ...*
>
> *Our goal was to have a hundred people in the book launch team and after we had told people that it was closing, but if they wanted to invite their friends, we ballooned up to 900 people in our prelaunch team. That was 900 people that had made a commitment to buy the book at the cheapest possible price, and get all the free stuff that went along with it, but also to leave a review.*
>
> *We tried to layer on if there's anything we could give to people to be a part of that team and we created a little*

Facebook group. We started promoting it, getting people to become part of that team, and then we did a, "Hey, there's a few days left to be partner of the book launch team. If you want to invite any of your friends, then now's the time. Here's the deadline...

"Right off the bat we had a good launch strategy and we got a bunch of people rallied behind the launch of the book and people that were committed ...

The book has grown in sales pretty much every month, maybe with one exception, but pretty much it's grown in sales every single month since it launched for the last year plus."

3. The Fortune Is In The Followup

Pat said that about 1/3rd of the people that agreed to participate in the launch actually followed though and left reviews on Amazon.

He also acknowledged, that this did not happen by accident.

One of the most powerful things he did, was to personally connect with and privately message every single person on this list.

*"About a third of those people actually left reviews. **I followed up with everybody.** I'm pretty good with fol-*

low up and pretty persistent. I had a list of every single person that committed. I was sending emails, following up with everybody that had left a review. I think if you want to really have the best launch possible, you've got to be willing to put in that kind of time to do that stuff."

One of the things I love about Pat, is that he's not afraid to do the work.

In this case, his "work" was to show his growing audience that he CARED about each and every one of them.

Pat's Advice To You:

To end the interview, I also asked Pat what words of advice he would like to share with the audience.

The big thing that Pat shared, is that having a book leads to BIG opportunities, and that it DOES NOT have to be as daunting or intimidating as you think.

Sure, it'll involve some work. Learning anything does. But once you do, the UPSIDE potential is incredible.

And, if you have a process, a proven system to follow - you can gain the CLARITY as to what to do first, what to do next, until you have an awesome book.

But the other thing I also LOVE, is that Pat, just like other multiple bestselling authors (Ryan, Ilona, and myself) believe ... is that if ONE BOOK can help you grow your business, having MANY books can help you CON-TINUE growing your business.

You don't have to be perfect. You get better by doing it over and over again.

RINSE. WASH. REPEAT.

This can create that GASOLINE on FIRE effect in your business over and over again.

> *"I guess I would say ... First off, I've definitely found that I never had any intentions of writing a book. It wasn't really on my goal list until Hal reached out. And like I said I thought it'd be a dumb thing to say no to and a great opportunity to give new talent, but one of the great benefits is that it definitely got me writing. It got me into that habit of writing. Now the idea of bringing a second book or a third book or whatever is much more on my radar. I'm deciding what those topics are. It's not nearly as intimidating as it was now, having gone through this process ...*
>
> *I guess that would be my main thing is why not do it? Even if your first book sucks, even if it's a learning experience, that's how you get good at anything, is that you'll learn all the ins and outs and the next one will be better."*

III - "Show Me The Money" Math

Pat was very forthcoming, by sharing his exact numbers during our interview.

In January 2017, Pat's book generated $18,000 in royalties from book sales.

Note, only get's half of the revenue from the book, because he shares the profits with his co-author, Hal Elrod.

On the backend of the book, Pat and Hal have grown a very engaged and loyal list of readers and fans that is now over 4,100 strong.

Pat is extremely careful to make sure he takes care of this list, and has made very few "offers" to them.

Again, similar to Ben, Pat is continually building goodwill, before offering his list an opportunity to buy from him.

This is a timeless success principle that I notice all successful entrepreneurs and business people have. They put the needs of their customers first.

Pat and Hal are not trying to just squeeze every bit of money and profit out of their growing audience. On the contrary, their goal is to add as much VALUE as possible, and to build BRAND loyalty that will last long-term.

Subsequently, Pat is building and growing a significantly more powerful asset than money.

To date, Pat and Hal have only generated approx. $20,000 in backend revenue from their growing list of fans/readers.

However, what's their upside potential as they continue to GROW and NURTURE their list?

Limitless.

Download and listen to the full interview: BigMoneyWithYourBook.com

SUCCESS STORY:

"One year, on vacation in Hawaii, I was relaxing at a beach, watching whales in the distance, when a fisherman, obviously a local, drove up in his pick-up truck. He got out with a dozen fishing rods. Not one. A dozen.

He baited each hook, cast all the lines into the ocean, and set the rods in the sand. Intrigued, I wandered over and asked him for an explanation. "It's simple," he said. "I love fish but I hate fishin'. I like eatin', not catchn'. So I cast out 12 lines.

By sunset, some of them will have caught a fish. Never all of 'em. So if I only cast one or two I might go hungry. But 12 is enough so some always catch. Usually there's enough for me and extras to sell to local restaurants. This way, I live the life I want."

The simple fellow had unwittingly put his finger on a powerful secret. The flaw in most businesses, that keeps them always in desperate need—which suppresses prices—is: too few lines cast in the ocean."

—Dan S. Kennedy, multi-millionaire, and author of the No BS book series

BIG MONEY MAKING IDEAS

NINE
How To Make 6-7 Figures With Your Book

"My mentor said, 'Let's go do it,' not 'You go do it.' How powerful when someone says, 'Let's!'"
— Jim Rohn

We aren't done yet.

My intention for this chapter is to help you select the path(s) you are going to take to make more money with your book. If you've chosen already, great. You can now lock 'em down, or add another strategy.

So far, Ryan, Ben, Ilona, Anil and Pat all shared the ways they used their book to make big money... five, six, seven figures and more.

I'm sure you've noticed some *overlap,* since a book can provide multiple income streams. Not all methods work for everyone, but hopefully, you've been inspired to pick your favorite strategies so you can get started right away.

To help you choose what might work best for you, I'm going to share FOUR simple methods, and why these might be good choices for you. I'll also crunch the numbers for you, so you can see exactly what it would take to turn these into 6-7 figures.

Let's begin.

MONEY MAKING METHOD #1
Online Product/Course

Everyone should have course.

My 9-year-old daughter even has an course for sale—and she wrote her first two books about *The 3 Ninja Kitties*.

So, when I say everyone, I mean everyone. Yes, you.

Even if you don't think you should offer a course or even if it feels like too much work.

Imagine selling something that once created, requires ZERO time, energy, or resources from you. Your client get's your awesomeness. You just sit back and get paid.

Now, if you're thinking, "But, I don't have a course." Or, "I don't have time to make a course or program!" Or, "How would that work for me?"

Consider the other examples in this book. If they can do it, you can do it.

Plus, here's the good news:

Your course can contain the same content as your book.

Sure it will have some *differences*.

But, think of it as a natural progression. A course is a natural extension that gives *even more* value than your book by itself. Yes, it'll be in a different format, but it is packaged in a way that people can more easily consume, apply and are willing to pay more money for.

Especially if they love you, your readers will want more.

Just in case you need any more evidence, let me share two more examples with you.

JESS TODTFELD

Jess wanted to finish writing and then publish his book.

When he and I talked about the possibility of having a course, Jess said he didn't have one, didn't have the time to make one, and really just wanted to just focus on finishing his book.

But instead of using these as excuses, Jess embraced the idea and chose to "pre-sell" his course during his book launch.

To be clear, when you "pre-sell" something, you're "selling it" before it's available for delivery, and often times before you create it. That's what Jess did. **He pre-sold a brand new course he hadn't created yet, and he offered it as an "upsell" during his *initial* book launch.**

What happened?

Within the first 24 hours of the launch of Jess's brand new book, *Media Secrets: A Media Training Crash Course,*

Jess not only became a #1 Bestseller, but he also made over a DOZEN sales of his brand-new $1,000 online course.

(To be transparent, I believe he offers a significant discount for the initial sales of his program, but within a month, he'd made over 30 new sales.)

How on earth did he make and find time to create his course?

Well, Jess delivered his course live, one day a week for 6 weeks. This way, he only had to work on one module at a time. Since the training was recorded, in just 6 weeks, Jess had created a course that was the perfect upsell to his book. Done.

Now, perhaps you might question the *quality* of a course created in this fashion?

Well, it was a hit. Jess' buyers LOVED his program and became raving fans. It has also become the foundation of a new "Certification Program," Jess is now offering his biggest and highest paying clients. He's so proud of the value and results his clients are getting, that the price for the course keeps going up...

To give you an example of the effectiveness of this strategy, Jess closed a $30,000 deal within months of the launch of his book. And, since this new client is an organization that is rapidly growing, that $30K will likely more than double within the first year.

All based on Jess's new course.

*[MORE ABOUT JESS: I've included a detailed case study in the BONUS CHAPTERS section for you: "**Bestseller Results In 24 Hours.**" This outlines the exact steps he used to successfully market his book, become a #1 Bestseller and promote his course at the same time.]*

Now I'll be honest, Jess is unique. Jess is also an absolutely awesome action taker. He's incredibly talented, and extremely good at creating transformational results for his clients. When people work with Jess, they get results. In this case, the result is they get MEDIA. Jess even guarantees that his clients will get results. He's fun, funny and makes the process of working with him enjoyable.

My guess is—you're awesome too.

But if you think Jess's results sounds too-good-to-be-true, then consider my 9-year-old daughter, Phoenix's story.

PHOENIX ROSE CRANE

Phoenix has written 9 books now, all of which have become bestsellers.

Since I keep shouting from the mountain-top that EVERY book, could and should have a business behind it, I had to get creative about the business we'd create behind my daughter's first book: *The 3 Ninja Kitties.*

In short, we decided to offer a course. The course teaches kids, and their parents, how to write books. My daughter knew how to do it , so she can teach it. She wrote it when she was 7, and became a bestselling author on her 8th birthday.

So SuperKidsBooks.com was born.

Now, on the back of every book, Phoenix promotes her website. She gives kids a chance to join her FREE Super Kids Book Club. And she promotes her mission to help 100 kids become *Super Kids Book authors.*

Let's do some "Show My 'Daughter' The Money" math.

Recently, my daughter decided she wanted to buy a new laptop. Cost: $1,000. I asked her how many "books" she needed to sell to make that much money.

At $10 per book, her answer was: 100 books.

Then, I asked her how many "courses" she would need to sell to make $1,000.

At $100 per course, her answer was: 10 courses.

I asked her which she'd rather sell. Her answer, God bless her, was **both**.

(I love that kid.)

If Jess can do it, YOU can do it.

If my 9-year-old can do it, YOU definitely can do it.

"Show Me The Money" Math:

You can charge as little or as much as you like.

But let's use an average price of around $1,000.

If you have a $1,000 course, and you get 25 people a month to buy that online course, the money starts to add up.

25 people a month, times a $1,000 = $25,000. Multiply that by 12 months, and you've got $300,000.

If you don't know how you'd find that many people or how to sell a course like that, it's okay. I didn't either, until I learned.

For now, just choose numbers you feel are appropriate for you, for your product or service. Maybe you charge a lot more, maybe you charge a lot less.

Let's say you only sold half, or even 10% of the numbers I used above. What would that extra income would mean to you?

And if you're thinking, "But Trevor, I don't have a product right now." That's okay.

That's part of what I can help you with. I can help you strategize about what that product should be, how it should be delivered, how to make it awesome, and better yet… how to get it done really, really, really fast.

Anyone can do it, and adding extra income like this, is a powerful way to monetize the back-end of your book.

Plus, if you have the book, then MOST of your online product/course is nearly completed.

That's why I think an online product is such a great example. If Ben and Ryan and Ilona and Jess and my daughter can do it...

You can too.

[MORE ABOUT PHOENIX: Find out more go to: SuperKidsBooks.com/author]

MONEY MAKING METHOD #2
Mentoring (Coaching or Consulting)

This is one of my favorite strategies, because it is one of the first things I chose to sell when I wrote my first book.

For years, coaching and consulting have been my primary source of income. There are few things more rewarding to me than working with people one-on-one, in groups, events and masterminds.

It's humbling and infinitely rewarding when you play a small part in the results you help other people create.

If you've not yet offered this type of service, I highly recommend it.

How much can you charge?

Most people start anywhere from a $1,000 a month to $10,000 a month, and even more.

"Show Me The Money" Math:

Again, let's just pick an average number that seems reasonable for coaching, which let's say it's around $2,500 a month.

If you got 10 coaching clients that pay you $2,500 a month.

Well, 10 x $2,500 is $25,000 a month. Multiply that by 12 months, and you've got $300,000.

Now, if you're not sure how to be a coach or offer consulting, don't worry. That's okay. I didn't either, until I learned. I enjoy this part of what I do so much, I'd do it for free.

Mentoring can also be one of the most leveraged ways for you to add extra income to your business. All without costing you a bunch of extra time.

In this example, you need 10 clients to earn an extra $300,000 a year.

Not bad.

In the past, loving something and getting paid for it didn't sit well with me and I stopped charging people. *Can you guess what happened?*

Unfortunately, since people value things based on what they pay for them. People didn't appreciate my help or advice NEARLY as much, as when I charged them for it.

If something costs them *nothing*, what's it worth? *Nothing.*

I believe very strongly that when people pay a decent sum of money for a course or program, the get better results.

In my first book *High Paying Clients*, I give people the "recipe" to sell high-ticket products and services. In the more expensive *course* and *mentoring* programs *beyond* the book, it's as if I appear in their kitchen and help them fry-up *success in a pan.*

Imagine two cars outside right now.

One is a $100 car. One is a $100,000 car.

Which would you rather own? Which would you rather drive? Which would you rather be "seen" in? Which one has more value?

(I've yet to meet anyone who "honestly" voted for the $100 car.)

Consciously, and unconsciously, we equate *value* with *price.*

MONEY MAKING METHOD #3: MEMBERSHIP SITE OR PROGRAM

How much can you charge?

You can charge as little, or as much as you like—again, it's up to you.

My wife and I have a monthly "membership" behind our **Revenue Accelerator Program**—or "**RAP**" for short. After this 8-week course, we transition people into a *hybrid* membership and coaching program for $297/month.

"Show Me The Money" Math:

Let's say you only charge $50 a month. Maybe you give away a free trial for 2 weeks or something, and then they upgrade to your monthly fee.

Let's just say you get 500 people enrolled in your course, and they're paying you $50 a month. Month after month. How much would that be?

That's $25,000 a month.
Or $300,000 a year.

SIDE NOTE:

I'm not saying that this stuff is *easy*.

What's important, is for you is to get "creative."

I always try to ask, "How can I do this?" Instead of, "Can I do this?"

You don't have to do them all at once. My suggestion is to start with **one**. Pick a price that you feel congruent charging, and figure it out.

> *"You don't have to be great to start,*
> *but you have to start to be great."* —*Zig Ziglar*

Maybe you charge less, maybe you charge more. It's up to you.

*Just in case you're not keeping track, **when you add those three income streams together, you'd have increased your annual income by $900,000.**

MONEY MAKING METHOD #4
MASTERMIND

This is another strategy I absolutely love and I believe offers massive value to your clients.

What is a "mastermind?"

The concept of a "master mind alliance" was introduced by Napoleon Hill in his book from the 1920s, *The Law of Success*, and expanded upon in his 1930s book, *Think And Grow Rich*.

These days, it's been shortened and modernized to just, "mastermind." Mastermind groups have been around since the beginning of time. Even Benjamin Franklin belonged to such a group, which he called a Junto. Napoleon Hill wrote about the mastermind group principle as:

"The coordination of knowledge and effort of two or more people, who work toward a definite purpose, in the spirit of harmony. No two minds ever come together without thereby creating a third, invisible intangible force, which may be likened to a third mind [the master mind]."

There's generally a mentor, or a group of mentors, that lead the group. Not only do you get personal access to the leader (or leaders) in the group, but even better you have access to other people in the community.

I'm a part of two masterminds, right now.

Masterminds can also be a ton of *fun*. The insights and assistance you get from the community is often "just as," or "more valuable than" what you get from the group's leader.

In the mastermind my wife and I have together we like to go on Mastermind Retreats. This year my wife is taking some of the women from her FEMM group to Cancun, Mexico. Later this year, we will take our clients on a trip to the Bahamas, where I use to live and work—and we're going to have a blast!

(I used to work for Royal Caribbean Cruiselines as a scuba instructor, and I've been looking forward to sharing the experience with my Mastermind clients for years. I lived on a small island about 1 and 1/2 miles long and 1/4 mile wide. I helped run the watersports on the island. This included: parasailing, snorkeling, scuba diving, spearfishing, sailing, kayaking, waverunner tours, and so much more.)

You'll often times find that **people get bigger faster results when they are part of a mastermind.** It's actually a little weird for those of us who are used to "working hard" for every dollar we make. In contrast, masterminds can be the most *laid-back* and *easiest* way to create results for people. *Because it's not solely up to YOU to help create results.*

But let's look at pricing. What can you charge for a mastermind?

"Show Me The Money" Math:

I've seen fees from $10,000 to a $100,000 to join a mastermind.

Let's say an average price point is $25,000.

Let's say that you just got 12 people in your mastermind.

12 people X $25,000 and you make another $300,000.

Now obviously, a mastermind is not for *everyone*. Not everyone who reads your book is open to investing that much with you. However, for certain people, **this is will be a perfect match,** and it opens the opportunity for you to do your **best and most transformational work with them.**

If you think the price for such a program is "high," consider what it "costs" people when they don't get the transformation they desire?

Sure, a mastermind often comes with a little bit of a higher fee—which is actually great for everyone. What I have found, is that when people invest more in themselves, half of your work is done. These clients will create bigger, better and faster results than anyone else you serve.

"When people pay, they pay attention."
—Trevor Crane

Period.

So, let's see, add up these numbers:

$300,000 Course
+ $300,000 Mentoring
+ $300,000 Membership
+ $300,000 Mastermind
= Total of $1.2 Million

Can you see the potential? Or, does it sound too unrealistic?

What if you only made half that? Or 20 percent? Or 10 percent? Or 5 percent?

It's your book, and your business. This book has given you a bunch of options.

The rest is up to you.

BONUS CHAPTERS

TEN

The Elf That
Stole Christmas

---

*"You have brains in your head. You have feet in your shoes.
You can steer yourself any direction you choose."*
—Dr. Seuss

Here's a little bed-time story about a little elf who is playing a mighty big game.

"In 2005, Christa Pitts left her job as a QVC host to help her mother, Carol Aebersold, and twin sister, Chanda Bell, to launch The Elf On The Shelf.

I don't remember a Christmas growing up without our elf, Fisbee. He would arrive every Thanksgiving. Each morning until Christmas Eve, my siblings and I would race out of bed to see where he was hiding. It wasn't until I got older that I realized no other families had that tradition."

In 2004, my mom was suffering from empty-nest syndrome, and my sister, Chanda, suggested that the two of them write a book together about Fisbee.

Every publisher turned them down.

I decided to quit my job and move back to Georgia to help them self-publish the book, which we planned to package with a toy elf. I was sure that other families would fall in love with the tradition, too.

To promote our first 5,000 units, we sent letters to every single person any of us had ever known.

A big tipping point came during the 2007 holiday season, when actress Jennifer Garner was photographed carrying an Elf on the Shelf box. Then the Today show ran a segment on us. That helped open doors with retailers like Barnes & Noble. Our products are now in more than 10,000 stores. We also have an animated Christmas special this year on CBS.

My mother, sister, and I are equal partners. We don't always agree, but we've spent our entire lives learning how to work through things together."

—Christa Pitts, Co-Creator Of The Elf On The Shelf

About The Elf on the Shelf.

Whether you find The Elf on the Shelf, cute, annoying or somewhere in between, he's everywhere these days. I've heard that some parents lament the creation, because it makes the holiday season even more complicated for them. Personally, I love it. Anything that grows the sense of love and magic in the world, and preserves the innocence and creative mind of my daughter wins in my book.

Did you know where this guy (or gal) came from, or who benefits from his shenanigans? Here are a few things you may not know about that elf on your shelf:

Where Did the Elf Come From?

What I love about this, is that it all started with a story and a book. It's a relatively new Christmas story and holiday tradition that started in 2005. The mother/daughter team, wrote the 'Elf on the Shelf' story. Despite tremendous setbacks they began their own publishing company. In the first year, they scraped together enough cash to make 5,000 of the $30 box sets and, after marketing them only at small festivals and events in Georgia and North Carolina, sold every last one of them. **The company has been growing ever since.**

What Has This Little Elf Done for His Makers?

The tenacity of the elf's creators has really paid off. Since the 2005 launch, the yearly growth of 'Elf on the Shelf' has averaged about 149 percent. Every year's increased production was paid for by profits from the year before. By 2011, sales had hit $16.6 million. The popularity of the little elf got a giant boost in 2007, when he was photographed with Jennifer Garner and the world wanted to know where she got him. The little elf has even won multiple book awards.

Where Else Can You Find Him?

Yes, you can find your shelf elf in random places around your home, but you can find him in other places as well. First of all, 2005 was not the first time scout elves were sent from Santa to watch over children. A company in Japan has been making "knee-hugger elves" since the 1960s, which were also sent from Santa to see who was being naughty and nice. So, you can find Elfie in Japan if you look. Since November 2011, you can find him in the Macy's Thanksgiving Day Parade. The sneaky little guy even appeared on television in 2011 when CBS aired a holiday special called 'The Elf on the Shelf: An Elf's Story.' Beyond that, little elves can be found in pretty much every corner of the Internet.

Sometimes He Can Behave Strangely

Basically, the elf's job is to sit there all day watching how kids behave. Then, at night he magically comes to life and heads to the North Pole to report back to Santa about what he saw. This is how he ends up in a different spot every day. Of course, the elf has a tendency to fight boredom by committing other strange and heinous acts while everyone sleeps—at least this is what we can tell from what we see on the Web. If there isn't another elf to keep an eye on your elf and report back to Santa, it appears that he will just do whatever he wants.

*Information featured in the article, "5 Things You Might Not Know About the Elf on the Shelf" By Kathy Landin December 16, 2013| http://allchristmas.fm/elf-on-the-shelf-trivia-things-you-didnt-know/?trackback=tsmclip

ELEVEN
Bestseller Results In 24 Hours

"Many have gone further and faster than they thought they would, simply because someone else believed they could."
—Trevor Crane

thought you might appreciate a bonus case study about one of our clients.

Meet Jess Todtfeld, bestselling author of *Media Secrets: A Media Training Crash Course.*

His book hit #1 in four countries in *less* than 24 hours. But that's not all. What followed were a DOZEN sales into his brand-new program, multiple requests to write, and be featured in major media around the country.

More MEDIA = More MONEY.

Below I hope you'll find some very actionable steps and methods to help you successfully market your own book.

SuccessInMedia.com

How Jess Hit #1

First of all, once Jess finished the "planning" and "strategy" phase of his book, we helped Jess plan out the next 12 months of his book-marketing-campaign.

The first phase was to offer his book for pre-order, or what we call a "Pre-Launch." This simply means that his book is available for sale on Amazon, before it is available to read, often before it's complete.

Think of this as if it's a "book advance" from a Traditional Publisher. Amazon is your publisher. They handle earthing and make your book available for sale immediately. You don't need a website, or a shipping cart or a business plan. But now, people can start BUYING your book before you have even completed it.

Then, these pre-sales accumulate in your Amazon bank account. This is money you're earn in advance of your writing your book. Then, Amazon gives you 90days to upload a viable version of your book.

*There's nothing like a deadline to help you finish your book.

You don't need to finish writing your book before getting the word out there! You can broadcast that you are writing one well beforehand.

Because it can lead to MORE BUSINESS, just like it did for Steve Napolitan. Just by telling people he was writing a book, Steve closed a $5,000 deposit for his services.

But let's get back to Jess.

Once Jess selected a DATE for this Pre-Launch, he planned a series of marketing communications to go out to the world. He planned his social media posts, he sent emails, he also solicited other promotional partners to help me "tell the world" to buy his book on Amazon, on his Pre-Launch day.

There are 2 very important things he did as well:

1. **As incentive Jess lowered the price of his book to $.99.** Remember, selling your book is NOT the MONEY MAKER. It's the BUSINESS off the back of the book that makes you money. For Jess, he sold his online course. By offering his book for only

$0.99, Jess also gained more purchases, which helps him gain BESTSELLER status faster!

2. **As an EXTRA incentive, Jess offered a special one-time-offer BONUS** for people to get his book TODAY. This is Jess offering INCENTIVE for people to take action immediately. He is offering MORE VALUE to his audience too. Just like Ben did, he put into play the practice of building *goodwill* with his audience.

So here is how Jess PROMOTED himself and BROADCASTED his message using social media (Facebook Live).

Figure 1 - Jess Using Facebook LIVE to Broadcast His Book

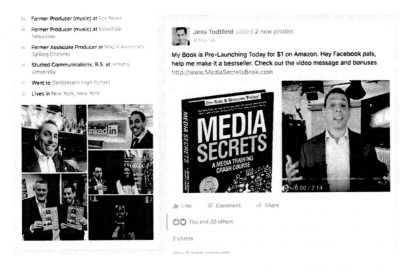

Figure 2 - Jess PRE-LAUNCHING His Book for a DIRT-CHEAP Price of $1.

How We Helped Promote Jess on Social Media

This is something I tell all my clients. Don't do it alone. Get PROMOTIONAL PARTNERS to help you BROADCAST your book. Since Jess was a private client of mine, he asked ME to be his promotional partner.

So I gladly obliged. Since HIM winning and killing it, does good for my brand too! See below, the MESSAGE I helped Tod broadcast using my Facebook and Twitter account.

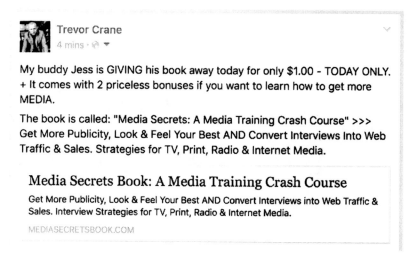

Figure 3 - Trevor Crane PROMOTIONAL PARTNER to Jess Todtfeld

Figure 4 - Trevor Crane's TWITTER BROADCAST for Jess Todtfeld

How Jess Made Over A Dozen Sales Into His New Course

Notice that the first thing Jess did, was he asked people to BUY his book. This is a important part of your own #1 Bestseller run.

Your #1 priority is to get people to buy your book TO-DAY (the day of your launch). That's how you get the NUMBERS up.

See the image below. It's what customers see when they click his link on Facebook (or the links on my social media broadcasts).

Figure 5 - PRE-SALE PROMOTION

But the next thing Jess did, was pure genius. (And we suggest you model it.)

As we mentioned, there was a secondary call-to-action, in this messaging. The 2nd thing Jess asked people to do was click the button to get their FREE BONUS. It's right below the "Click here to BUY the Pre-Order $1 Today Only."

Once someone clicked this link, they were asked to enter their email, to get the bonus (see below).

Figure 6 - NAME and EMAIL Capture Form

THIS IS A VERY IMPORTANT PART OF YOUR MARKETING

You need a LIST of people who like your stuff. So you can CONTINUALLY interact with them, give them VALUE, build *goodwill* and make SELL them your product or service.

Okay. Let's carry on.

The "Thank You" video on the next page, then described a very special, and limited one-time-offer to pick up Jess's new course at a discount.

Figure 7 - THANK YOU Page and UPSELL

Do you see what just happened? He made an offer for them to buy something.

By the way, he DID NOT HAVE A COURSE ready for them. And he didn't pretend he did. He told people on the video, that he was going to offer them a brand-new course, that he would create with them during a series of LIVE trainings.

Do you see what just happened? He sold something first. And he decided to create it later. He didn't hide this fact, he celebrated it.

There is ALWAYS an invitation for the customer to take the NEXT STEP.

Figure 8 - The PURCHASE PAGE for His PAID MEDIA COURSEs

The Results

According to Jess, about 400 people visited the first page of this "funnel" to get his book. (More people bought his book, but not through this funnel.)

Of those 400 people, approximately 25%, or 100 people, clicked the link to get the bonuses. About 15 percent or 14 people, took him up on his offer to buy his program.

Awesome!

Sure, if Jess had it to do over, he could have easily made his BONUS and his SALE more sexy, and improved his conversions and his sales... but in less than 24 hours, BEFORE his book was written, Jess made more money than he paid for the entire program he purchased from us (the Bestseller Big Business Academy + Bestseller Big Business Mentoring programs).

In addition, Jess also promoted a LIVE Broadcast, in the middle of his Pre-Launch Day to help build extra value and create some buzz for his book, and upcoming new program. The value he positioned was a free Q&A with him.

Media Secrets - Live Broadcast with Jess

Sign into the webinar using the name & email you registered with.

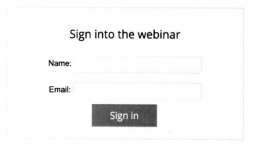

Sign into the webinar

Name:

Email:

Sign in

Thank You. You're All Set!
Check your email. We sent you all the info.

An Exclusive Online Webinar hosted by Jess Todtfeld

A couple of steps to get ready for the webinar...

Step 1: Add this webinar to your calendar by clicking the "Add to Calendar" button on the right.

Step 2: Share this webinar with your friends below!

See you on the webinar!

Share this webinar!

Powered by : WebinarNinja

How Jess Got Media Attention During His Launch

So there were a few more things Jess did, during his launch that you might want to model.

- **He asked promotional partners to help him promote his book,** and asked them to email their lists, and ask them to get the book, on his pre-launch day. Correct, I was NOT the ONLY promotional partner he had ☺

- **He exported his contact list from LinkedIn**, and then uploaded them to an email service that allowed him to email his LinkedIn list, that his book, and bonus were coming out. (Yes, you can do that!)

- **He also emailed his extensive list of Media Contacts**, (TV, Radio, and Print) that his book was coming out. After all, he is full of MEDIA SECRETS. So he was practicing the material he teaches!

Now can you do ALL of these?

Sure. You just need your own: Partners, List of Contacts, and Media Connections. (If you don't have those lists, that's okay. At one point, Jess didn't either.

However, one of the things we give you access to in our Bestseller Big Business Programs: Academy+ Mentoring… is access to Partners, Contacts, and Media Connections, so you can run your own promotion similar to Jess.

As a result of this promotion, Jess received 2 offers for him to write a column for 2 publications, and he got multiple requests to be a featured guest on both online (Blogs and Podcasts) as well as traditional offline media (TV, Radio and Print).

Plus… here are some pretty cool #1 Bestseller screenshots Jess got from Amazon.

(Which at the time I'm writing this, have stayed at #1 for almost a month.)

The AWESOME Amazon Results

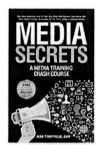

Media Secrets: A Media Training Crash Course Kindle Edition
by Jess Todtfeld ▾ (Author)

› See all formats and editions

Kindle
$0.99

Read with Our **Free App**

Strategies for Getting the Most From TV, Print, Radio, Internet & Social Media Opportunities. The most up to date media training book on the market. The idea of Media is more than just TV, Print, and Radio. Media now includes social media interviews, Skype, Periscope, Facebook Live, Blog interviews. It means Leveraging Traditional and Internet Media. All are important. Includes "Media Training Quick Start" Free Audio Download "Jess Todtfeld is a media training expert." —The Washington Post

Word Wise: Enabled ▾   Enhanced Type

   SaneBox: Clean up your inbox in minutes
Learns what email is important to you and filters out what isn't -- saving you hours Try it FREE

Editorial Reviews

About the Author
Jess Todtfeld is President of Success In Media, Inc, one of the leading business communication and media training authorities in the U.S. With more than 2 begin with one simple question...
"*What Are You Trying to Create More of?*"
Todtfeld has spoken for, or consulted clients from, the United Nations, IBM, JPMorgan, AARP, USA Today, The World Children's Wellness Foundation, Land I Producer on the National Level for networks including NBC, ABC, and FOX. During that time he booked and produced over 5,000 segments.
He was also part of the team that launched "The O'Reilly Factor" and "Fox & Friends." On the other side of the camera, Todtfeld has hosted, reported, and s

Product Details
File Size: 1782 KB
Print Length: 6 pages
Simultaneous Device Usage: Unlimited
Publisher: Bestseller Big Business Publishing (October 5, 2016)
Publication Date: October 5, 2016
Sold by: Amazon Digital Services LLC
Language: English
ASIN: B01I2JJHH2
Text-to-Speech: Enabled ▾
X-Ray: Not Enabled ▾
Word Wise: Enabled
Lending: Not Enabled
Enhanced Typesetting: Enabled ▾
Amazon Best Sellers Rank: #50,491 Paid in Kindle Store [See Top 100 Paid in Kindle Store]
  #1 in Books > Reference > Writing, Research & Publishing Guides > Writing > **Newspapers & Magazines**
  #1 in Kindle Store > Kindle eBooks > Humor & Entertainment > Radio > **General Broadcasting**
  #1 in Kindle Store > Kindle eBooks > Humor & Entertainment > Television > **Direction & Production**

Media Secrets: A Media Training Crash Course Kindle Edition
by Jess Todtfeld ▾ (Author)

‹ See all formats and editions

Kindle
$0.99

Read with Our Free App

Strategies for Getting the Most From TV, Print, Radio, Internet& Social Media Opportunities. The most up to date media training book on the market. The idea of Media is more than just TV, Print, and Radio. Media now includes social media interviews, Skype, Periscope, Facebook Live, Blog interviews. It means Leveraging Traditional and Internet Media. All are important. Includes "Media Training Quick Start" Free Audio Download "Jess Todtfeld is a media training expert." ---The Washington Post

Word Wise: Enabled ▾   Enhanced Typ

Barron's
Outsmart the market with Barron's digital membership. Only $12 for 12 weeks › Learn more

Amazon Best Sellers Rank: #50,491 Paid in Kindle Store (See Top 100 Paid in Kindle Store)
#1 in Books > Reference > Writing, Research & Publishing Guides > Writing > **Newspapers & Magazines**
#1 in Kindle Store > Kindle eBooks > Humor & Entertainment > Radio > **General Broadcasting**
#1 in Kindle Store > Kindle eBooks > Humor & Entertainment > Television > **Direction & Production**

Would you like to give feedback on images or tell us about a lower price?

More About the Author

› Visit Amazon's Jess Todtfeld Page

+ Follow

Biography

Jess Todtfeld is President of Success In Media, Inc, one of the leading business communication an question...

"What Are You Trying to Create More of?"

Todtfeld has spoken for, or consulted clients from, the United Nations, IBM, JPMorgan, AARP, USA National Level for networks including NBC, ABC, and FOX. During that time he booked and produc

Show More

Amazon Best Sellers
Our most popular products based on sales. Updated hourly

‹ Any Department
  ‹ Books
    ‹ Reference
      ‹ Writing, Research &
        Publishing Guides
        Writing
          Academic &
          Commercial
          Children's Literature
          Editing
          Fiction
          Journalism &
          Nonfiction
          Newspapers &
          Magazines
          Play & Scriptwriting
          Poetry
          Technical

Best Sellers in Newspapers & Magazines Writing Reference

1.

Media Secrets: A Media Training Crash...
by Jess Todtfeld
Release Date: October 5, 2016
Kindle Edition
$0.99

2.

Writer's Digest Handbook of Magazine...
by Michelle Ruborg
★★★★½ (43)
Hardcover
99 used & new from $0.01

3.

Writer's Digest Handbook of Short Sto...
by Jean M. Fredette
★★★★½ (12)
Paperback
129 used & new from $0.01

Amazon Best Sellers Rank: #50,491 Paid in Kindle Store (See Top 100 Paid in Kindle Store)
   #1 in Books > Reference > Writing, Research & Publishing Guides > Writing > **Newspapers & Magazines**
   #1 in Kindle Store > Kindle eBooks > Humor & Entertainment > Radio > **General Broadcasting**
   #1 in Kindle Store > Kindle eBooks > Humor & Entertainment > Television > **Direction & Production**

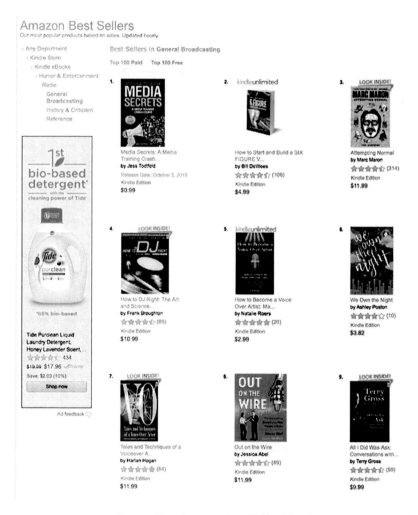

Figure 11 - Amazon Best Sellers Rank

If you take anything away from this post, I hope it's this — you can have a **BIG launch**. You can **become a #1 Bestseller**. You can make this part of your long-term marketing strategy to get your book in as many hands as possible, and use it as **your most powerful marketing tool** — for the business behind your book..

Making a great book that people want to buy, and having marketing machines set up to encourage more sales, beyond your book is what will ultimately lead to your success.

I've seen it over and over. It's not magic; it just takes the right plan, and some hard work.

I struggled for years on my own, to create results like these. It is my mission and my purpose to help you, in any and every way that I can. Everything that I do is designed to help you sell more stuff, have more fun, and be more successful.

There's always another level, and I can't wait to help you get there!

BIG MONEY
PROGRAMS

I - FREE TRAINING TO BECOME AN AUTHOR

If you don't have a book yet, or you want help writing your next book, I'd like to give you this audio training 100% FREE.

The Proven Path To Become An Author in 90 days or Less

FREE TRAINING

Make this the year you "finally" write your book!

BestsellerBigBusiness.com/free

II - BESTSELLER ACADEMY

This is my life-changing online course which is a 3-part program designed to walk you step-by-step with everything you need to get your book done, and how to use it to SELL your products and services ...without stopping what you're currently doing or wasting time.

- WRITE a great book – faster than you ever dreamed possible

- MARKET it a #1 bestseller guaranteed – plus a 12 month promotion plan

- MONETIZE it and add an extra 6-7 figures to your business

TrevorCrane.com/bbbacademy/

III - BESTSELLER MENTORING

This is a 6-month journey we will take together to transform your book, your business and your life. (Perfect for business owners, authors, speakers, coaches, consultants, and entrepreneurs.)

All we do is create bestsellers and build the big businesses behind them.

TrevorCrane.com/bbbmentoring

*Results described in this book are not typical.

I AM IN NOW WAY MAKING PROMISES THAT "YOU" WILL CREATE SIMILAR RESULTS.

Most people are not willing to follow through. Most people won't do what it takes. Most people would rather make excuses, than create results. I don't know you, your business, your skills, strengths, weaknesses, opportunities or limitations. For all I know you'll do nothing with this information.

What I do know, is that it's possible.

The rest is up to you.

ACKNOWLEDGEMENTS

cannot even begin to express how grateful I am for all of the people who came into my life exactly when I needed them most. Your life-changing wisdom and belief in me, supported me when I didn't believe in myself.

Thanks to my wife, Robyn Crane for tolerating me even when I make incredibly stupid decisions, like publishing 10 books in 90 days. Thanks to my daughter for being soooo awesome—because five of those books were yours. You are so sweet and so talented, we are the luckiest parents in the world to have you in our lives.

Thanks to Ashley Peterson, who my wife describes as being "our everything." Without you, we would have only a fraction of our success. (And it wouldn't be nearly as fun.)

Thanks to Jon Low, and our entire publishing team her at Bestseller Big Business Publishing. You helped me get things out of my head, and heart, and onto paper so that it could change peoples lives.

Thanks to all of my teachers and mentors, and the people who have blazed the trail ahead for me and everyone else in the world. (Including: Mike Koenigs, Ed Rush, Chandler Bolt, Rob Kosberg, Jack Canfield, Mark Victor Hansen, Robert Kiyosaki, Tim Ferris, Seth Godin, Grant Cardone, and so many more.)

Thanks to Tony Robbins.

You helped brain wash me, when I was in desperate need of a bath. Everything changed for me, for the better. While you hardly know me, you've been a close friend to me. You've always there to give me great advice (through your products and programs) and when I speak with you out loud to myself like a crazy person, (having both sides of a conversation with you). And, you chair the head of my imaginary CIA Round Table that I keep in my head. (CIA = my Central Intelligence Agency)

Thanks to all the authors I love.

You are too numerous to list specifically here. But you inspire me. You entertain me. And I could't imagine living without your books.

Thanks to you, the reader.

I write my books for you.

I hope you use this one to change the world.

ABOUT THE AUTHOR

"A mentor is someone who allows you to see the hope inside yourself."
—Oprah Winfrey

struggled for over 20 years to write my first book. I'm not proud of it. But it's true. I had ideas for books, and spent time journaling, and doing research for different book ideas. I wasted years.

But, for one reason or another, I just couldn't get a book done.

Fast forward to today. I'm a ten-time #1 international bestselling author. I spend my days helping people build their ideal business, so they can live their ideal life. I help them publish and profit from their books, and share their message and their mission with the world.

My team and I specialize in creating products and programs that help entrepreneurs create phenomenal business success. In 2014 alone, my team and I **helped our**

clients generate *more than* $13 million dollars in bottom-line profits.

"Profit" is what's left after you pay all your expenses. It's what you take home and buy bacon with. Or veggie-burgers… whatever you're into. Oh well, I guess after Uncle Sam takes his cut. So, it's after *THAT*… but it's money in "your" pocket.

I feel very fortunate to have been blessed to help make a *difference* in people's lives worldwide. That's the most important thing to me in the world—that, and my family and my friends. That's what matters to me most.

But having this type of abundance wasn't the norm for me. It's taken a lifetime of work, monumental mistakes, and trial, error, success, failure, set-backs and so forth…

I was born the son of a horseshoer in Phoenix, Arizona.

Growing up, my family struggled to put food on the table and pay the bills. Our family slogan seemed to be "We can't afford it." My parents fought about money a lot. We didn't have extra money to buy nice things. We didn't take vacations.

Then, when I was 7 years old, just after I my great, great, grandfather had passed away, I found out that, *at one point,* our family had *millions* of dollars.

With a growling stomach, I looked around me and wondered where all that money went.

I found out that, subsequent generations had *blown* all the money. Hearing the story, I decided then and there that I would figure out how to make millions and rebuild the family fortune. That's been a goal of mine, ever since.

But it wasn't all sunshine and rainbows. I found myself building up some success, only to lose everything—*twice.*

The most painful experience was when I filed a 2.2 Million dollar bankruptcy in 2009.

The most painful part was losing my 2 year old daughter. Her mom left me, took her and left the state.

I sold everything in my house that wasn't bolted down, and even sold some things that were. I dug up plants and trees from around my yard and sold those—I sold EVERYTHING I could.

At possibly my lowest low point, I gave away my dog, Mojo, to a friend, because I didn't have a place to live. Fortunately, I had friends who let me stay with them. I moved from basement, to attic, and from couch to couch.

One of the hardest parts of it all was the feeling that no one would ever trust me again, because I was convinced that I was...

A Loser

In that state, it felt as though I was the last person in the world, any one would ever want to take advice from. Let alone, did I think I could ever be an author. *Who would anyone ever want to read one of my books?* I wouldn't wish "losing everything' on my worst enemy.

I made a series of poor decisions. Then worse ones.

I refused to accept the help and mentoring of others. I was stubborn. I thought I knew it all, but inside I knew I was a fraud. And I kept thinking that I "should be" smart enough to figure it all out by myself.

I blamed others for my problems. I started fights. I sued the people who had "wronged" me. All of this without really looking in the mirror, and facing the truth. Staring back at me was the guy *ultimately responsible* for where I ended up.

But finally, I started getting it right.

I stopped blaming others. I accepted that I had actually been the cause of all of my problems. The great thing about that was, while I couldn't control other people, I could take charge of myself.

Over several years, I rebuilt my business and my life.

I sought out new mentors. I found the fortitude to push through challenges, or better yet, I got insight from people who cared about me and were smarter than I was, so I could avoid problems in the first place.

Yet, while it worked. It still wasn't great.

I was very busy putting in a lot of effort for little return. ***But, when I finally became an author, everything changed.***

Instantly, my positioning shifted. The trust and authority I was trying to **PUSH** down peoples' throats, was now nearly automatic. I stopped having to work hard to convince people to work with me.

Instead, people were *attracted* to me. They wanted to work with me.

But I want to be clear; it wasn't "only" my book.

It was *everything*.

It was everything I'd gone through. It was my mindset, the mentoring, and the MAP's (Massive Action Plans) that my new circle of influence gave me.

But, here's also what I found:

The problems and pain are part of the process.

Our Setbacks Are Setups For Success.

Today, my life is as about as abundant as life can be.

I'm passionately in love with (and married to) *Robyn Crane*, the woman of my dreams. My daughter *Phoenix* and I spend our time playing, having fun and writing books. The three of us love being c-r-a-z-y and have adventures together.

Little Miss Phoenix Rose Crane, is a 9-year-old 9-time bestselling author. She also starred in a movie she wrote called *Kitty Wars*. My daughter co-founded Super Kids

Books Publishing with me, and is on a mission to help 100 kids become Super Kids book authors.

I'm more proud of my daughter an her accomplishments that anything I've ever created.

Today, instead of struggling to get by, we give back, and we volunteer our time and donate to the charities we love most.

I don't share this to brag. I'm just proud of the life we have and, quite honestly, I cherish it, because it wasn't always this way.

But no one who succeeds at anything great, does it alone.

I believe you need the right mentoring, mindset, and the right MAP to succeed.

But also, it can be as easy as changing the "music" you're listening to.

Ever get a song stuck in your head? Maybe you hum it all day. Maybe you hear it when you go to sleep at night. Maybe you made the colossal mistake of going to Disneyland and getting on the ride whose tune follows you around for days, "*It's Small World after all...*"

This is similar to the inner-monologue that goes on in our heads. It talks to us about our abilities, and our expectations.

But when you change the music, when you choose to tune into *different* **input**, you start to focus on things differently, and you get *different* **output**.

If you aren't getting the results you want, maybe all you need to listen to is, a new tune.

I hope this book has been the right tune for you.

More Books by Trevor Crane

TrevorCrane.com/books

CPSIA information can be obtained
at www.ICGtesting.com
Printed in the USA
LVOW10s0511200717

541972LV00032B/1100/P